SCIENCE POLICY
AND BUSINESS

The Diebold Institute for Public Policy Studies, Inc.

T HE John Diebold Lectures are made possible by a grant from The Diebold Institute for Public Policy Studies, Inc., a nonprofit foundation established by John Diebold in 1967. The Institute functions on the dual premise that those concerned, even indirectly, with bringing about the application of scientific and technological change should also concern themselves with the human and social implications of that change, and that society's response to this problem has been inadequate. The private nature of the needed response to what is essentially a public policy problem is a basic consideration of the Institute's activities.

Among the programs initiated by the Institute is the development of a series of monographs on the social and managerial problems of technological change. These monographs are being published as part of the Praeger Special Studies in U.S. Economic and Social Development. Another program is the sponsorship of the John Diebold Lectures at Harvard University, a joint effort of the Economics Department and the Graduate School of Business Administration, which seeks to bring to the Harvard community distinguished administrators of scientifically based enterprises to explore the interaction of technology and management. Another program is a three-year research project on the "Business-Public Sector Interface," the objective of which is to determine what specific business contributions to public sector activities will be meaningful for the public.

The first series of John Diebold Lectures was presented at the Harvard Business School in 1968–1970. The second series was held on December 9, 1971, at The Hague, The Netherlands.

SCIENCE POLICY AND BUSINESS

The Changing Relation of Europe and the United States

The
John Diebold
Lectures
1971

David W. Ewing
Editor

HARVARD UNIVERSITY
GRADUATE SCHOOL OF BUSINESS ADMINISTRATION
DISTRIBUTED BY HARVARD UNIVERSITY PRESS
Boston 1973

Contents

iv

Foreword

THE SECOND series of The John Diebold Lectures was held at The Hague on December 9, 1971. Made possible by a grant from The Diebold Institute for Public Policy Studies, a nonprofit foundation established by John Diebold in 1967, the Lectures were designed to enable men and women of substantial and distinguished experience in industry and government to discuss the implications, opportunities, and challenges for management of scientific and technological change. Like the first series on "Technological Change and Management," held between 1968 and 1970,* the second series was offered by the Harvard Business School in cooperation with the Department of Economics of Harvard University. His Royal Highness, The Prince of The Netherlands, served as Patron of the meetings.

The program was a unique one — a departure in several ways from its predecessor. The audience at the Hotel Wittebrug, where the sessions were conducted, consisted of about 100 people, all personally invited because of their eminence in business, government, science, journalism, and other professions. They, the speakers, and the panelists, about whom more will be said presently, represented an extraordinary combination of talent and experience.

Surely there is no need here to review the highlights of the lectures, panel discussions, and audience-speaker dialogues. The

---

* The proceedings were published in book form under the title, *Technological Change and Management*, edited by David W. Ewing (Boston, Harvard Business School, 1970); available from Harvard University Press, 79 Garden St., Cambridge, Mass. 02138.

participants speak for themselves, and the reader will find no trouble in getting to the heart of the arguments presented. However, those who peruse this volume have an advantage that those who attended the sessions did not. Here one has more time to stop and reflect; he does not have to keep pace with the speakers and the clock. And in this more leisurely setting one can, I believe, ponder a development which, though never explicitly discussed at the second series of Diebold Lectures, nevertheless pervades the discussions from first to last, continually seeming to hover in the background, like a large and invisible presence.

I refer to the emergence of a multipolar world. The two-polar world of the first two decades or so following World War II is a thing of the past. We are now in a "brand new ball game." The United States and the Soviet Union are in this game but no longer dominate it. Europe is now in it. Japan is now in it. The People's Republic of China is on its way in. What was once a two-team race for industrial and technological leadership is a four-team race exploding into a five-team race.

Repeatedly, this new reality is acknowledged by the contributors to this book. In the morning session, the main speaker analyzes the declining technological gap between the United States and Europe, concluding that it will continue to narrow. Despite their contrasting backgrounds and interests, *every* panelist accepts this proposition. Europe is indeed catching up — and catching up to stay — all agree. Moreover, there seems to be widespread agreement that the forces reducing U.S. superiority have a sort of universal quality about them; they will operate on Europe and Japan too — increasingly as competitors from those areas draw head to head with the American corporations.

At the luncheon session, a Japanese executive makes it clear that Japan, now it has become a leading power, is not satisfied with the catch-up strategy it has been following during the past 20 years. Japan's strategy is now to become a go-ahead nation. It wants to innovate. It seeks to develop leadership in areas of basic technical theory so that, at least in some lines of technology, *other* nations will be cast in Japan's accustomed role of borrowing, adapting, and emulating. In other words, in a contest where the players are truly well matched, each gets ahead now and then; each has an edge on the others in certain areas.

And then in the afternoon session the new reality receives perhaps the frankest recognition of all. No longer is it a case of Europe defending itself successfully against the American challenge, the participants indicate. In the multipolar world of today, Europe is more and more on the attack, not just the defensive. It gives tit for tat, invading the U.S. market just as American companies invade its market. There are differences of opinion as to how best to do this — whether to start small in the U.S. market and attempt to grow big gradually or start more ambitiously, whether to invade by means of joint ventures or takeovers, and other questions. But that European multinational companies can do it and are doing it, and will do it ever more successfully in the future — of this there seems to be no doubt.

Is the emergence of a multipolar economic world a benign development or a portentous one? Only time will tell. But in these lectures, panel discussions, and dialogues one can pick out many of the elements that will ultimately combine in some way to answer that question. The contributors to this volume are practical men but also far-seeing men. Working as they do at the centers of power in industry and government, they feel the pulse of a new economic system, hear the drum beat of a new technological march. They know from doing how the new reality is changing decision making, planning, goal setting, and thinking ahead.

Who are these men? How did they pool their contributions to the program? Let us look at the agenda.

Lawrence E. Fouraker, Dean of the Harvard Business School, opened the proceedings at 9:30 a.m. Following his introduction and a question-and-answer period, the Chairman of the morning session, Lord Zuckerman, former Chief Scientific Advisor for the

British Government, introduced the first lecturer, Dr. Harvey Brooks, Dean of Engineering and Applied Physics at Harvard University.

After Dean Brooks had delivered his paper, Lord Zuckerman reviewed it and turned the proceedings over to a four-man panel composed of John B. Adams, Director General of Laboratory II, CERN; Lord Bowden, Principal, The University of Manchester Institute of Science and Technology; Professor Umberto Colombo, Director of Research for Montedison; and Dr. Gerhard Stoltenberg, Minister President, Schleswig-Holstein, and former Minister of Science of the German Federal Republic. Having studied the Brooks paper in advance, each of these authorities delivered a short commentary on it. What did they consider to be its most important points? Where did they agree with Dean Brooks — and where did they disagree? What further ideas did they find worth adding?

Next Lord Zuckerman invited the audience to participate. What questions did the lecture and panel discussions raise in their minds? A short, interesting dialogue ensued between the speakers and members of the audience. Then Lord Zuckerman asked Dean Brooks to give a summing up, and the morning session ended.

Following luncheon and a welcome from His Royal Highness, Prince Bernhard of The Netherlands, Dean Fouraker introduced the next speaker, Sohei Nakayama, President of the Overseas Technical Cooperation Agency of Japan. Mr. Nakayama, who is also a director of the Japanese Development Bank and of the Japan Productivity Center and a member of the advisory committee of the Japanese National Railways, analyzed his country's remarkable achievements in economic growth and described its changing strategy.

At 3:00 p.m. the afternoon session began, with Dean Fouraker acting as Chairman. He introduced the opening lecturer, Dr. Kurt Richebächer, Director of the Dresdner Bank AG. Following this paper, another panel took over, this one composed of

A.W.J. Caron, Vice Chairman of Unilever, Gianluigi Gabetti, General Manager of the Istituto Finanziario Industriale, and G. Kraijenhoff, President of AKZO. (Georges Hereil, former Chairman of Simca-Chrysler, had been scheduled as a fourth panelist but was unable to participate.) The panelists reflected on the major themes of Dr. Richebächer's lecture, pointed out significant implications, and added facts and observations from their own experiences.

Again the audience was invited to participate, and again the floor enlivened the program with a diversity of challenging questions and viewpoints. The lecturer and panelists responded, sometimes with facts or clarifications of their positions, sometimes with new questions. The proceedings were adjourned at 5:30 p.m.

This book represents an attempt to capture the most important points presented during the full and active day of December 9, 1971, at The Hague. The proceedings were taped and transcribed in The Netherlands; Janet Bowers and I then edited the transcripts for printing by the Harvard University Printing Office. Particularly in the case of the extemporaneous talks and question-and-answer dialogues, we have tried to preserve the qualities of spontaneity and responsiveness that marked the proceedings; at the same time, we have pruned various parts of the transcript in order to avoid redundancy, edited the text throughout to make it more readable, and occasionally added headings and footnotes for the sake of clarification. Some of the questions from the floor have been deleted.

This volume is the product of many people's efforts besides those of John Diebold, the contributors, and my own. Janet Bowers of the *Harvard Business Review* editorial staff, already mentioned, did considerable editing and handled much of the production effort. Liesa Bing, a vice president of The Diebold Group, lent a helping hand at many points along the way. Marian Kirchner, also of the *Harvard Business Review* staff, took care of a great deal of correspondence, checking, and other office work. Kathy Schwartz converted hundreds of pages of marked up, often hard-to-read transcript into clear, readable copy for authors and printer. Peter Imrie and his associates at the Harvard University Printing Office did their usual fine job of printing and binding.

David W. Ewing
Executive Editor–Planning
Harvard Business Review

Soldiers Field
Boston, Massachusetts
August 1972

1

Opening Remarks

By LAWRENCE E. FOURAKER

Dean, Graduate School of Business Administration, Harvard University

I T IS especially appropriate to have an exchange of ideas and viewpoints about science policy and business in The Netherlands. This kind of exchange has always been viewed here as an activity important to the improvement of human conditions. We at the Harvard Business School share that philosophy. We believe that trade and the exchange of ideas, educational experiences, and philosophies are appropriate and creative. We hope that belief is ingrained in the action and behavior of our graduates.

I want to discuss the question of the Harvard Business School's interest in Europe and our plan for extending and expanding our activities on this continent. There has been a great amount of speculation about this plan among the academic communities in Europe — and there has been some misinformation about it.

Let me explain the decisions we have made in historical sequence. I became Dean of the School about two years ago. One of my first problems was to respond to an exponentially increasing series of requests from our Faculty to teach in short executive programs in Europe. This flood of requests was generated by an increase in the number of European business schools that also was exponential. There are now more than 50 business schools in Europe. They typically have small faculties.

The desire of these schools to have Harvard Business School instructors teaching Harvard materials in short executive programs was so great in the aggregate that we would not have had anyone left to teach at Soldiers Field if I had approved all of the requests. Being unable to differentiate among them, I did not approve any, on the assumption that it would be inappropriate for our Faculty to teach in competing educational programs.

But it is quite impossible, of course, to keep Americans in America. Columbus established the precedent: upon discovering the place, he immediately returned to Europe. That is the repeated pattern, I think, of all of your families that have come to the United States. They return. Accordingly, I placed a very small probability on the prospect of an absence of Harvard teachers from Europe for very long. The questions before us were: How should our Faculty be represented in Europe? Under whose auspices should they teach?

We saw two alternatives. First, Harvard teachers might go to Europe in a series of small entrepreneurial efforts, not unknown in our Faculty, where they would teach short programs of their own design, using U.S. teaching materials, and by this means finance pleasant holidays on the Continent. Each country would receive dubious educational benefits from such programs — I have serious reservations about them. They are little more than introductions to what we try to do at the Harvard Business School. Teachers and students cannot achieve very much in a week. Also, I think it is late in the century to attempt to teach European businessmen about business management, using American materials exclusively. This is true even for Europeans who are interested primarily in expanding into the American market.

The alternative approach we considered was to construct one program under the School's auspices. Our objectives would be to develop appropriate teaching materials for that program from Europe, Japan, and other industrial countries around the world; to have the courses directed to managers who either had or shortly would have very broad responsibilities in large international organizations; and to attempt to ensure that the quality of such a program was up to the standards of excellence that we have always tried to maintain at Soldiers Field.

The second approach was the one we elected and are pursuing today. Our aim is to ensure that any educational activity identified with Harvard, either formally or informally, is of high quality — both abroad and in the United States. It is important to bear in mind that we have an increasing number of Europeans enrolled in each of our programs at Soldiers Field. I am convinced that we can no longer maintain the quality of our edu-

4

cational effort in Boston by relying primarily on American teaching materials.

Let me give you a few figures on Europeans in our various educational programs:

— We have had over a thousand continental Europeans graduate from our Master of Business Administration (MBA) Program.

— The Advanced Management Program (AMP) has had more than 640 Europeans.

— Our Middle Management Program for people in their thirties has had more than 300 graduates from Europe.

— The International Teachers Program (ITP) that we have conducted for a number of years (the last two years in Lausanne, Switzerland, under the chairmanship of Professor Frank Aguilar) has had nearly 200 graduates; 196 European teachers of business administration have gone through that 12-week program or some predecessor version of it.

— Our Doctoral Program at the present time has 31 Europeans enrolled; nearly half of them are from France.

All told, more than 2,000 Europeans have gone through our various programs at the Harvard Business School. These people typically intend to return to their native countries to practice management. In years past many of them went into debt to such an extent that they would have to work for an American corporation for a few years to reduce the debt to a manageable proportion before they returned home. But now rising salaries in Europe have closed that gap (we speak of many gaps today!), and most Europeans who come to the School return immediately to their national origins.

The problem of any business educational effort is to relate knowledge and action in some way. Our conviction is that knowledge must yield to the requirements of action. Usually in a practical setting action requires a time limit — it is by next Tuesday that a decision must be made. A manager does not have time to collect all of the research that is available, much less undertake new research, to solve a problem. He must collect what information he can through whatever mechanism is at his disposal, and make a decision after that information is gathered that can be sustained in the interests of his organization. This is in contrast to the more traditional academic concept of a philosopher king who does not undertake royal action until he has mastered philosophy; and since mastery of philosophy is a lifetime pursuit, presumably he is not able to consider issues of importance until he nears the end of his career.

If we try to transmit skills, they are not technical skills of the day as much as they are skills drawn from a very diverse group of people in a Harvard classroom. They include knowing when to make a contribution, how to get in and out of a conversation, how to aggregate the accumulated wisdom and experience of the group, how to defer to a course of discussion that seems to have the support of the group even though one is convinced that his own view may be superior. Basically these are skills of resolving conflict in an organization; if mastered, we think, they can be an important asset to a managerial career.

The approach followed by many other institutions — lecturing from a disciplined base and leaving it to the student to integrate the disciplines and relate the knowledge of practical problems of the world — is useful. I think that it is complementary to the Harvard Business School approach, and one should not displace or replace the other.

Sometime in 1973 we plan to offer an executive program to Americans and Europeans interested in large international organizations, somewhere in Europe. We would be delighted to do so in conjunction and collaboration with a European institution or a combination of such institutions. We are quite convinced that some collaborative effort should take place; in fact, the mechanisms for that have already been started, as the European institutions have formed a discussion group in response to the Harvard announcement of last June. We are talking with many of the people affiliated with institutions that have strong Harvard ties — institutions that in their inception or later development received the interest, support, and concern of Harvard Faculty members. Often they drew their deans, presidents, or teachers from Boston, and I hope they will continue to do that in the future.

Admittedly, cooperation and collaboration are difficult with institutions sensitive to their relationship to an older and larger parent organization. But I am persuaded that collaboration *can* be accomplished and *should* be accomplished. We are coming to Europe, not to compete or to weaken business education on this continent; that would be quite against the stream of our efforts for the last 50 years. We come to Europe to reinforce its business education, to learn as well as teach, and to collaborate through the series of programs that I have described. For example:

○ The International Teachers Program is going to have a series of workshops in 1972 under the direction of Professor Frank Aguilar.

○ We will support and encourage a European clearing house of case materials. Our form of education requires a very expensive and continuing effort to describe problems that are of practical importance, and we need some mechanism to ensure that the cases are widely distributed.

○ We will encourage collaborative research and course development.

M. Pierre Massé, both an academic and a manager, and a man who exemplifies the combination of knowledge and action that would be our objective in our new program, has said: "The basis for rapid expansion is a continued redistribution of work and capital, assuring their application to the most productive ends at all times. This mobilization of resources, which everyone recommends, implies a mobility that many refuse. It is no longer enough to agree to isolated changes separated by long slack periods. We must learn to live in the midst of accelerating change."

This state of constant receptivity, this need to be accommodating, comes as a shock to many. Changes can be deeply unsettling to those who have to give up their old ways. They are going to be unsettling for many Harvard people.

I am quite certain that the MBA will have a different role in the European organization from the one he has enjoyed in the American organization. Also, it may be that he should have a different role in the American organization. Professors Ray Vernon and Bruce Scott of the Harvard Business School, who are engaged in research on the Continent, have persuaded me that the European international company is a very different organism from the American international company. Their tentative conclusion, based on their studies in Japan, is that the Japanese international company is not the same as either the European or American. These differences, I think, are desirable; information about them should be exchanged broadly.

A.W.J. CARON (UNILEVER).

May I just ask whether you have already decided on the content of your European program, how long it will be, and how similar it will be to the program at the Harvard Business School? We in international business would, of course, like very much to send our sons to a Harvard program in Europe, and I think if you go on to middle management and advanced management courses, there also are quite a few of our employees who could benefit from your program. If you move in this direction, the quicker the better, I would think, so that all of us will become part of one world, not necessarily the Harvard world, but one world in which education will be on the same level.

DEAN FOURAKER.

We have not decided on a specific program, Mr. Caron. I have been working with a group of Faculty under the chairmanship

8

of Professor Aguilar on curriculum questions. As for the length of the program, it will be between six and ten weeks. We will not offer anything comparable to an MBA program in Europe; our intent would be to start with senior managers around the age of 40 in the short program.

The composition of the Faculty group might well include one or more European teachers. The planning and design of the curriculum could be a joint activity with one or more European Faculties. About one third of the Harvard Faculty have spent at least a year abroad, teaching or doing research in foreign settings, and almost that many of our Faculty were originally nationals of countries other than the United States. We have Dutchmen, Belgians, and Frenchmen on our Faculty. We probably could offer a course in one of those languages. However, I expect all courses will be in English, inasmuch as that seems to be a common currency. Our notion would be to start this program quickly, as we are convinced we have a product of high quality.

BOHDAN HAWRYLYSHYN (CENTRE D'ETUDES INDUSTRIELLES, GENEVA).

I want to comment as a member of one of the European institutions you mentioned. First, we very much appreciate the desire and the need for Harvard Business School to internationalize itself. We feel this need is very much the same as it is for firms; it would be difficult for you to be significant in the future unless you go international. Secondly, we at CEI have experienced a period of growth. In four years we have moved from 50 participants to 500 per year. We have multiplied our revenue by a factor of five. We certainly want to see here in Europe truly multinational educational efforts, not just foreign branches of well-known national schools.

We also see that there is some wisdom in trying to develop truly indigenous institutions that are an organic outgrowth of a given country or continent. There is a period in which an infant

9

industry needs some protection. I think the Japanese have shown the wisdom of that by holding off the taking over of some of their business institutions by foreign interests. They have done remarkably well to develop their own institutions, and now they can confront anybody in the world on anybody's terms.

2

Have the Circumstances That Placed the United States in the Lead in Science and Technology Changed?

By HARVEY BROOKS

Dean of Engineering and Applied Physics,
Harvard University

A MOST remarkable and swift change in the climate of opinion has occurred in the United States over the last four years with respect to our attitude toward science and technology and toward our relative technological standing in the world. In this presentation it will not be my purpose to diagnose the causes of the change but, rather, to assess the underlying realities and the degree to which the change in public perception reflects a change in the real world and should be considered an accurate harbinger of things to come.

As late as 1967, many American and European opinion leaders would probably have accepted the following five propositions:

1. There is a technology gap between Europe and the United States, and this gap is steadily widening to the latter's advantage. The gap will lead eventually to Europe's becoming an economic and technological colony of the United States unless Europe can overcome the inertia of its traditional institutions and combine the efforts of its diverse national groupings more effectively to meet the U.S. technological challenge.

2. The technology gap is primarily the result of large U.S. governmental expenditures for research and development in defense, space, and nuclear energy. These expenditures have resulted in an enormous technological spin-off for civilian industry, which has given it a great advantage in international trade, made possible large investments in high-technology production in Europe by American companies, and generated a dynamic U.S. economy.

3. The U.S. technological lead is accompanied by, and in part due to, its superior performance in virtually every significant field of basic science. Its scientific leadership is steadily increasing in degree and comprehensiveness.

4. A prime source of the U.S. lead in science is the superior system of graduate education in the U.S. universities, combined with the system of research grant support of individual profes-

sors, in which projects are chosen on the basis of open national competitive evaluation by committees of scientific peers in the same or closely related fields. The project grant system has fostered a creative scientific entrepreneurship which stimulates greater originality in science and more rapid identification and exploitation of potential applications of basic science.

5. The United States is experiencing a severe shortage of scientists and engineers in almost every category, leading to a continuing and even accelerating immigration of foreign scientists, engineers, and doctors. This so-called "brain drain" is the result of the superior capacity of the U.S. economy and system of higher education to utilize scientists and engineers effectively.

But now almost the direct converse of each proposition is being asserted — most insistently in the United States, but to some extent in Europe as well. Let me summarize them in the same order:

1. Europe and, most visibly, Japan are overtaking the United States in the export of high-technology products, and many European and especially Japanese products are displacing their American counterparts in world markets. At the same time these nations are showing an even more evidently superior performance in low-technology industries, whose exports are taking over U.S. markets.

2. The concentration of R&D in a narrow range of sophisticated technologies for defense and space, in the United States, has diverted innovative talent and energy as well as venture capital away from civilian industry and from public needs other than defense and national prestige. The high demand for the most creative technical and managerial talent generated by government programs in the space and defense sectors has raised the cost of innovation in U.S. industry compared with the cost to its principal competitors.

The resulting discouragement to innovation in all but a few industries has been a major factor in the deteriorating U.S.

14

trade balance, especially in products derived from mature technologies. In other words, the spin-off from space-defense spending, especially R&D spending, has been largely a negative factor in the economy.

An exception is a very narrow range of sophisticated technologies, such as computers and jet aircraft, generated directly by the government. Although important for our trade balance, these technologies contribute relatively little to our GNP and cannot be expected to offset indefinitely the rising trade deficit in almost all other product areas, and in raw materials.

3. Although the United States still enjoys a lead in many areas of basic science, this advantage is disappearing as the federal government withdraws its support of graduate training and research. In the meantime, research support in other nations continues to climb steadily and in some instances rapidly.

Owing to declining support, the growth of anti-intellectualism and antitechnology sentiment among students and the public, and the increasing preoccupation of research sponsors in government and industry with short-term payoffs from research, the morale of the U.S. scientific community is at an all-time low. It has lost confidence in itself and in the future of American science.[1]

4. Both inside and outside academic ranks, there is serious disenchantment with the system of graduate training in science. Industry sees it as too narrow and specialized, and too remote from the real-world problems with which technical people in industry must cope. Many students and the public see graduate education as irrelevant to the most pressing problems of the modern world and the system itself as "elitist" and self-serving, designed to exploit students and the public purse for the greater personal glory of professors.

At the same time, the system of project support is viewed as corrupting the intellectual integrity of professors, destroying in-

1. See my article, "Can Science Survive in the Modern Age?" *Science,* October 1, 1971, p. 21.

stitutional loyalty, and eroding the quality of teaching — thus constituting a prime cause of student unrest. The professors themselves see the project system, insofar as the funds come from mission-oriented agencies with no firm responsibility to education, as a major source of the instability and variability in the funding of basic research.

5. In almost all fields of science, there is a surplus of Ph.D.s which the academic institutions should have foreseen. It will grow steadily worse throughout the 1970's unless drastic steps are taken to curtail graduate programs and discourage students from entering graduate work — or perhaps even higher education.

Industry expresses satisfaction that it no longer is forced to compete as heavily with graduate schools in recruiting the most talented and most motivated students. Instead, it can bring them directly into its own laboratories before they have been "spoiled" by the attitudes inculcated in the graduate schools.

Where the Truth Lies

How much has really changed in less than five years to convert the first five propositions to their opposites? In my view, reality is much more complex than these propositions, and has changed more slowly than the perceptions. Things were not so good before, nor are they so bad now. Both sets of propositions are caricatures.

Let me try first to summarize very briefly where I think the truth lies:

1. It is clear that the technical and economic inferiority of Europe in the early post-World War II period was unnatural and was certain to be overcome as soon as reasonably favorable social and economic conditions returned there. The technology gap is closing and probably has been closing since the mid-1950's, at least.

What we are seeing, in fact, is the emergence of an increasingly *international* science, technology, and economic system in which the very concept of superiority and inferiority has less and less meaning. It seems most likely that the industrialized countries as a group are approaching some sort of saturation relative to past growth, and the United States, as the most advanced nation in per-capita GNP, has entered the transition phase a few years in advance of its competitors.

Other industrialized nations will likely continue to close the gap, but they will gradually approach the same approximate level as the United States rather than pass it on a steeply rising curve. Of the factors in the United States that have slowed the growth of science, generated the reaction against technology, and produced the disenchantment with productivity as an economic objective, many are visible also in other advanced countries.

2. The current diagnosis of the impact of space-defense R&D on innovation in the rest of the economy is probably essentially correct. The United States is long overdue for a period of "catch-up" in other areas, a change in priorities toward civilian technology. This seems to be foreshadowed in pronouncements from both political parties.

Although research has given the United States a foreign trade advantage in computers, aircraft, industrial electronics, and a few other advanced technologies, other nations have been able to purchase technology from us in these areas while utilizing their own technical manpower on a broader industrial front. At the same time they have enjoyed the extra incentive that always accompanies a number two position. This incentive will tend to disappear as Europe and Japan catch up.

3. These judgments on "leadership" apply also, to some extent, to basic science. In this area we are dealing with an even more internationalized system, in which knowledge and talent move with ever-increasing freedom. Surprisingly, productivity in science correlates closely with GNP, and the U.S. contribution to

world science will tend to decline proportionately as its share of world GNP declines, but probably no faster.

Antirational and antitechnology trends in the United States do not appear to be having a major impact on the number of college graduates in science, or on the attraction of the highest talent to science.

Restorative forces operating against cutbacks of government research support are likely to make themselves felt soon, while the European surge in science and graduate education will probably slow down. Symptoms of this slowdown are already appearing. Europe and Japan are both benefiting from the dynamism and relatively high elan that go with expansion, while starting from a smaller base.

4. The superiority of U.S. graduate education over European has probably always been somewhat exaggerated. Despite the many criticisms, I think the U.S. system is basically healthy. (Europe and Japan are moving more towards its pattern.) It is highly adaptable, and *is* adapting to new priorities. But the time lag produces a feeling of crisis.

A convergence between the European and American support systems for science is also detectable. Unless the United States adopts a "protectionist" policy with respect to the movement of its scientists (for example, by restricting money for foreign travel), competition is likely to make all educational systems increasingly alike.

5. The present "surplus" of scientists and engineers in the United States is the product of the coincidence of several factors: the cutback in research-intensive space and defense activities, the economic recession, and the financial crisis of higher education.

While there is little likelihood of a return to the Ph.D. shortages of the 1950's and 1960's, I believe the present surplus will work itself out through expansion of the career opportunities considered appropriate for Ph.D.s, stabilization or a slight contraction of the output of graduate schools, and a relative reduction of the salary levels of scientists and engineers to bring supply and demand into better balance. At the same time, the rapid expansion of European higher education is likely to lead to similar "surpluses" there within a few years.

The growing array of social and environmental problems developing in all advanced societies as a result of continuing economic growth is likely to result in a new demand for scientific and technological effort by the 1980's and 1990's, perhaps comparable in intensity to the post-Sputnik demand. This development, combined with a shrinkage of the talent pool available for advanced technical training — due to population changes — will produce a general shortage of scientists and engineers.

The Technology Gap

Richard R. Nelson has shown that the technology gap is not new, that it has in fact existed and been growing since the last quarter of the nineteenth century.[2] Joseph Ben David has put forward similar arguments.[3] Analyzing 50 major industrial innovations of the twentieth century, originally presented as case studies by John Jewkes, David Sawes, and Richard Stillerman, Ben David shows that 32 were initiated wholly or partly in the United States and 38 brought wholly or partly to final commercial application in the United States. In 1962, the United States paid only $61 million to other countries for technological knowledge and received $577 million in payments for such knowledge.

Moreover, the favorable trade balance in patents, royalties, and so on, had increased to $743 million by 1968.[4] It was this

2. "World Leadership, the Technological Gap, and National Science Policy," *Minerva*, July 1971, p. 386.
3. "Fundamental Research and the Universities: Some Comments on International Differences" (Paris, Organisation for Economic Cooperation and Development, 1968).
4. See C. Freeman and A. Young, *The Research and Development Effort in Western Europe, North America and the Soviet Union: An Experimental International Comparison of Research Expenditures and*

information about the balance of trade in know-how that triggered the political furor over the technology gap. The United States has for a long time shown a superior capacity to convert research results, from whatever source, into commercial products.

Yet at the very time that the technology gap was receiving the most attention in government circles, the seeds of change were germinating rapidly. Although from 1870 to 1950 the annual rate of growth of productivity in the United States exceeded that in Europe or Japan, the situation began to change after 1950 (see *Exhibit I*). Since 1965 the inferior productivity growth in the United States has worsened considerably. In Europe during this period it was nearly three times that in the United States, and in Japan, six times. From 1960 to 1970 labor productivity in the United States grew only 35%, while that in Japan grew 188%; in West Germany, 74%; and in the supposedly laggard United Kingdom, 40%.

Exhibit I. Average Annual Productivity Growth

	1870–1950	1950–1965	1965–1969
United States	2.4%	2.6%	1.7%
Europe	1.5%	4.0%	4.5%
Japan	1.4%	6.8%	10.6%

In 1968 the estimated value of the total civilian technology effort, including the capitalized value of purchased foreign technology, was 1.6% of GNP in the United States, 3% in Japan, and 3.6% in West Germany.[5] Thus it appears that since at least

Manpower in 1962 (Paris, Organisation for Economic Cooperation and Development, 1962), pp. 51–55 and Table 6, p. 74; and J.W. Wilcox, "New Technology and Trade," *Supporting Studies for Alternate Federal Policies Affecting the Use of Technology*, NSF Grant GQ–5, pp. 193–218 and Table 3, p. 202.

5. House Science and Astronautics Committee, "Science, Technology, and the Economy," Hearings in the 92nd Congress, July 27–29, 1971 (U.S. Government Printing Office, 1971), and testimony of Secretary Maurice Stans, Chart 7, p. 13.

the middle of the 1950's the technological position of Europe has been improving from an overall point of view relative to that of the United States. It is only in the more spectacular military-space technologies that the United States has been clearly ahead, and in the closely associated civilian technologies. The relative improvement of the technological position of Europe is also revealed in statistics of the U.S. Patent Office, which show that foreign patent applications filed in this country have been rising much faster than domestic patents.

The general situation in technological effort is now being dramatically reflected in trade. Although our net trade balance in high-technology products is still favorable overall by $9 billion, it is negative with Japan by $1.1 billion, favorable with Europe by about $2.4 billion, and favorable with the rest of the world exclusive of Canada by $7.4 billion. Thus 77% of our trade surplus, even in high technology, is with the less-developed world.

These figures may be somewhat misleading because sales of U.S. manufacturing subsidiaries abroad, most of them in high-technology areas, are more than twice exports.

When one considers low-technology products — those from industries in which R&D is a low percentage of sales — the unfavorable position of the United States becomes quite dramatic. Exports and imports of such products last balanced in 1958, and since that date the excess of imports over exports has risen to $6.1 billion. Agriculture, which is really a high-technology industry, has shown a steady surplus of $1.4 billion to $2 billion, while raw material imports have exceeded exports at a steady $2.5 billion to $3 billion, a gap that is projected to grow rapidly in the next decade.

The turnaround in low-technology products has been very rapid. As one example, iron and steel went from a surplus of $160 million in 1960 to a deficit of $760 million in 1970. Even some nominally high-technology products, such as automotive products and parts, television and radio, and phonographs and sound reproduction, have shifted into the deficit category, in magnitude about 30% of the 1970 net surplus. Although nominally high-technology, these products represent the maturer segments of their industry, where the pioneer's comparative advantages have largely been lost.

Most economists believe that rates of return on R&D investment considerably exceed those on investments in fixed capital, and that most productivity growth is accounted for by technological change rather than by quantitative growth in capital and labor. Of course, the two are not really separable, for in a rapidly growing economy or industry, new knowledge can be incorporated more rapidly in new equipment and in the training of a growing labor force. In the United States, rates of savings and of investment in fixed assets have averaged less than half those in Europe and one third those in Japan, when measured relative to GNP.

Nevertheless, there is considerable evidence in support of the proposition that the deterioration of the U.S. trade balance reflects a comparative deterioration in its technological performance, particularly in the more mature low-technology industries. Furthermore, this deterioration has been going on for some time.

The U.S. government is beginning to act on this hypothesis, responding by some expansion and more talk of direct and indirect subsidy of industrial research. Secretary of Commerce Maurice Stans made a clear statement of such a policy last year to the Science and Astronautics Committee of the House of Representatives:

"The magnitude of the problem is such that we cannot rely upon normal forces to maintain our advantage in technology. We are at the forefront in many technological areas. The costs of breaking new ground in some of these areas are high — higher than private companies or perhaps even private consortia are able to justify because the risks are so great.

"We have recognized this fact in space, defense, and atomic energy areas. Other trading nations have recognized it in the area of civilian R&D and have taken steps to assist technological development. If we are to maintain our advantages in this area, we must first of all accept the idea that it has become a proper sphere of government action."[6]

Figures gathered by the Organisation for Economic Cooperation and Development (OECD) indicate that public R&D expenditures in support of economic objectives in agriculture and manufacturing, as a fraction of all public R&D expenditures, are considerably lower in the United States than in almost all other Western nations. Some typical figures are shown in *Exhibit II*. Even on a gross national basis, private and public, we spend a smaller fraction of R&D on economic objectives and on academic science than any other industrialized, non-Communist nation, although this is due more to the great emphasis on R&D in military objectives than to low total expenditures.

Exhibit II. Percentage Share of Public R&D Expenditures That Support Economic Objectives in Agriculture, Manufacturing, and Services, 1968–1969

United States	6.0%
Canada	48.9
United Kingdom	22.1
France	16.5
Japan	25.0
Sweden	13.1
The Netherlands	18.0

Space-Defense Outlays & Spin-Off

As time goes on, space and defense technologies become more specialized and esoteric, and hence more remote from potential civilian applications. In the 1950's, military aircraft developments were easily adapted to civilian jet transports; solid-state

6. *Ibid.*, p. 17.

circuitry could be adapted for consumer electronics; business computers could be derived from missile-guidance computers; military radar could be readily adapted to air traffic control or weather radar; satellites for telecommunications could be boosted into orbit with the earliest and most modest boosters.

But the computer required for the Safeguard ABM seems to transcend any that would have a business or even a scientific application. It is unlikely that the Apollo space vehicle will be used for commercial transportation in the near future. Furthermore, numerous studies suggest that the incidental "fallout" of technology from space and defense work has been relatively small when compared with expenditures. Such fallout as has occurred has arisen mainly from the more generic and basic aspects of the research rather than from the design and development of specific end items, where much of the funding has been concentrated.

The two generic technologies resulting from space and defense work, solid-state electronics and computers, now have many civil applications. Emphasis on development of laser technology for defense applications will also undoubtedly accelerate the application of this basic technology in important civil areas, but the total amount of defense R&D in this case is very small compared with the major development programs.

Possibly much of the fallout from the space-defense research of the 1960's is yet to appear, as adaptive research gradually exploits the existing pool of knowledge. Hence all the economic return from this research may not yet have been realized. But I doubt whether the future fallout will change the basic picture; even the unrealized benefits of space-defense R&D are most likely to derive from evolution and elaboration of generic technologies.

On the other hand, there is little question that the great demand on a limited pool of scientific and technical manpower, especially between 1954 and 1962, considerably disrupted the manpower market. J. Herbert Hollomon and A.E. Harger have documented the fact that this demand raised the salaries of scientists and engineers not only directly but also by upgrading technicians to engineering responsibilities.[7] They estimate that more than 100,000 people without technical degrees became engineers during this period, mostly in the aerospace industry. Today it is these people who are somewhat overrepresented among unemployed engineers.[8] During the period 1958 to 1965 more than 75% of all the new R&D employment of scientists and engineers occurred in two industries, aerospace and electronics. Hollomon and Harger estimate that by the mid-1960's salary levels of technical persons were 30% higher relative to general wage levels in the United States than they had been in the early 1950's.

The problem, however, was not one of price alone. The technical challenges presented by space and defense programs were often much more interesting than those of civilian industry and attracted more than their share of the best talent and the best-trained people, quite apart from salary. The result was to overprice the innovation process in these programs. This overpricing was a prime factor in the lag in civilian technology and the gradual deterioration of the U.S. trade advantage. It is not surprising that the lag particularly affected the low-technology or mature industries, whose innovative investments tend to be most sensitive to economics.

If this theory is correct, the negative fallout of space-defense research owing to overpricing of innovative activity may have far outweighed the benefits from the crumbs of technology dropped from the national security and prestige table.

Part of the current unemployment among scientists and engineers in the United States is apparently the result of this overpricing. The rapid decline in government defense expenditures

7. "America's Technological Dilemma," *Technology Review*, Vol. 73, No. 9, 1971.
8. National Science Foundation, *Science Resources Studies Highlights*, Washington, NSF 71–33, September 23, 1971, p. 1.

has caused a lag in the adjustment of the salary structure to the new market, resulting in underemployment of resources.

Declining Support of Basic Research

The United States has never included support of research as an integral part of its system of support for higher education. The spectacular increases in support of academic research since World War II have been largely a political accident connected to the arms race and to the massive political appeal of health programs. They were not the result of a coherent policy for higher education or a firm national consensus concerning the value and importance of basic research to the nation's economic and social health. Even biomedical research is now succumbing to pragmatic subservience to short-term goals.

Since its peak in 1966, federal subsidy of academic research has probably declined in real terms by close to 20%, and this has occurred during a period when graduate enrollment and total faculty population were still increasing substantially each year. At the same time, during the early and mid-1960's, major investments were made in new basic research facilities, especially in nuclear and elementary particle physics and in oceanography. These investments were made in the expectation of increased funds to operate the facilities and to support the work to be done in them. When these funds did not materialize, the resulting underemployment of resources was more acute than absolute dollar figures alone would suggest.

The ensuing demand on funds to support work with frontier facilities could be met only by closing down numerous smaller, though still productive, research efforts — efforts which tended to be much more labor-intensive than those at the large facilities. Thus the declining support picture was greatly aggravated in manpower terms.

But decline in support may be less significant in the long run than other factors, such as lowered public esteem for science and scientists; disenchantment with technology and, by association, with science; insistence on short-term or easily demonstrable "payoff" from research efforts; and a growing feeling among some scientists that many of the worthwhile fundamental discoveries have already been made.

Graduate Education

Both the praise and criticism of graduate education are probably exaggerated. The U.S. graduate education system has expanded enormously since 1960, and undoubtedly there has been some deterioration in the quality of the graduates being turned out. The major stress has been placed on new programs or ones previously of very small size.

An allied effect has been the increased "homogenization" of higher education in the United States, with more and more institutions trying to imitate the goals and style of the pace-setters. There has been a tendency for every institution to try to do everything, with the same emphases as other institutions; hence less institutional differentiation and division of labor. More science and engineering Ph.D.s and M.D.s as a proportion of their age group were produced in 1970 than *bachelors* in science and engineering in 1920.

But the pattern is now undergoing change. Graduate schools of arts and sciences are losing popularity, especially in the sciences and engineering, while medical schools and law schools are almost ridiculously oversubscribed, in part because they appear to offer superior opportunity for immediate social action.

Graduate education in science and engineering, especially the latter, has tended to be coupled best with the industries that received the largest government R&D support in the 1950's and

1960's, aerospace and electronics. There is now a feeling that in many fields of basic science the frontiers have advanced so far ahead of industrial and general economic needs that they are becoming increasingly isolated from society.

This has undoubtedly been one of the factors in the softening of the market for science graduates outside of academia. Thus science and graduate education are no longer sustained by the "pull" of society, a situation which is particularly difficult in this country, where support of both science and education has always relied to such a large extent on a pragmatic rationale.

A recent poll of academic scientists and engineering faculty documented the extraordinary pervasiveness of self-doubt and disillusionment about the whole education and research enterprise that exists even in the most prestigious ranks of academic science. For example, more than 60% of those surveyed agreed with the proposition that professors exploit their graduate students to advance their own research and prestige; nearly 50% felt that the most successful professors were "operators" rather than scholars; and more than 30% said that large research grants "corrupt" their recipients.[9]

Unfortunately, we have no data on past opinion, say, ten years ago. There is also no assurance that the results of this type of survey reflect the realities of the academic scene, as has often been demonstrated in similar polls. But there certainly is a question as to how long American science can survive as a vital and forward-looking enterprise if the disenchantment and cynicism among scientists are as widespread as they seem. What is especially disturbing is the evidence of loss of confidence in the self-regulating and self-policing mechanisms of the scientific community, evidenced by the apparent belief that external recognition and prestige no longer necessarily go to the most creative scholars or to the most important intellectual contributions.

9. S.M. Lipset and Everett C. Ladd, "Politics of Academic Natural Scientists and Engineers," paper presented at annual meeting of the American Political Science Association, Chicago, September 7–11, 1971.

In the United States, the coincidence of three factors has conspired to produce a severe impact on the employment of Ph.D.s, as well as all scientists and engineers. The situation has hit most severely in the physical sciences, especially physics. But it extends to all fields, although there are isolated specialties, such as computer science and systems analysis, that still enjoy a fairly good employment market. The factors are:

— The cutback in government space and defense spending and the general slackening of support for research, especially academic research. The fraction of the federal budget devoted to R&D has dropped by about 40%, and the percentage of GNP in R&D has dropped from a maximum of 3.04% in 1964 to 2.79% in 1970.

— The very rapid increase in output of Ph.D.s in almost all scientific fields in the last decade. To achieve this output required a rapid expansion of faculty, which in turn increased the demand for Ph.D.s to fill academic positions. A sudden slackening of external demand has produced a slackening of academic demand as well, which is further aggravated by the financial crisis of the universities brought about in part by inflation and in part by federal government policy.

— General slackness in the economy, with the result that the industries providing the largest job market for scientists and engineers are either not expanding or are actually contracting. Much industrial R&D is closely associated with the rate of new capital investment, which is very low in the United States, compared with Europe and Japan, and which is especially vulnerable to economic stagnation.

A general factor is the relationship of the new social priorities to areas of economic activity that traditionally are less research-intensive than space, defense, and nuclear energy. In the latter three areas, R&D accounts for more than 15% of the total economic activity, while for the economy as a whole the figure is only about 3%, and much less for the maturer industries.

Full utilization of the current R&D volume, redeployed for civil purposes, would imply an enormous expansion in growth or a transition to a much more research-intensive style of doing things in both the private and public sectors. But this transition may require a long learning period before research can be really productive. Just such a long transition period was required in the military field, where in the prewar period the military mind was regarded as a synonym for technical backwardness.

The federal government's civilian R&D activity is expanding at a high rate, but it starts from such a small base that it can compensate for only a small percentage decrease in the space-defense areas. Growth is slowed by the different mix of skills needed. The effective utilization of research in a new area of application requires the rather slow and painful creation of new institutional mechanisms and linkages between technical people and ultimate users, linkages that are not ensured by the mere generation of the necessary science.

Part of the present adjustment is due, as I have indicated, to overpricing of scientists and engineers relative to current domestic demand and relative to competitors of the United States. A price adjustment is now taking place, especially in starting salaries of Ph.D.s. For example, starting salaries of chemists fell 7% in 1971,[10] and all professional and technical salaries have fallen relative to the general wage levels during the last two or three years. The price adjustment is expected to lead to fuller utilization of scientists and engineers within a few years, since the evidence suggests that price elasticity of demand is very high for technical effort.

On the other hand, the percentage of high school graduates in the 21-year-old age group who obtain college degrees in natural

10. Paul Doty and Dorothy Zinberg, "Science and the Undergraduate," draft paper for the Carnegie Commission, edited by Carl Kaysen, November 1971; estimate attributed to R.B. Freeman.

sciences has remained remarkably constant and independent of external influences for many decades. Changes in demand tend to cause shifts only between disciplines, not between natural science and other areas. Doctorates in science, medicine, and engineering account for 40% of all college science and engineering graduates, so the system is nearly saturated on the supply side, regardless of what happens to demand. Some expansion could come from greater participation of women and racial minorities, especially the former, but this is likely to be slow because of the deep sociological changes required.

Other parts of the world are likely to grow more than the United States in science, if only because their potential pool of sufficiently talented manpower is much further from exhaustion. This will undoubtedly mean some deterioration in our relative position, even if we had no problems of financial support.

On the other hand, neither graduate nor undergraduate enrollments in science in this country confirm the pessimistic picture sometimes given of a wholesale "flight from science." As a group, potential scientists are apparently highly inner-directed and respond only marginally (for example, by shifting from biochemistry to medicine, from chemistry to biology, or from physics to mathematics) to external influences. The drastic cultural shift predicted by some indicators appears to be less deep-seated than its superficial manifestations suggest, and perhaps it is confined to institutions that enroll mostly upper-middle class students.

Summing Up

I believe that the United States is experiencing only a few years earlier some of the forces and trends that will become worldwide among industrialized countries: saturation of the demand for scientists and technologists, competition of social welfare and other public expenditures for the government budget, increased public preoccupation with the undesirable side effects of technology, disenchantment with science on both the right and the left of the political spectrum, and increased preoccupation of society with equality rather than excellence.

Furthermore, the scientific system is increasingly international, so that the very concept of national superiority in science or technology is becoming obsolete. It will be harder and harder to tell who is "ahead" or "behind" as frontier science is conducted in multinational institutions like CERN and as technology is introduced and diffused by international corporations that will become truly multinational and identified less with particular home countries.

The United States will never again enjoy its enormous superiority of the first half of the 1960's, but neither is it about to be overtaken dramatically by Europe or Japan. Rather, we are all approaching a common asymptote, which will probably represent a condition of slower growth, both in science and in the economy at large, than we have been accustomed to in the recent past.

Dean Brooks's address was followed by a discussion of its main points. Lord Zuckerman, former Chief Scientific Advisor to the British Government, chaired the discussion. After summarizing the principal ideas in Dean Brooks's paper, he introduced the four discussants:

John B. Adams, *Director General, Laboratory II, CERN*
Lord Bowden, *Principal, The University of Manchester Institute of Science and Technology*
Umberto Colombo, *Director of Research, Montedison*
Gerhard Stoltenberg, *Minister President, Schleswig-Holstein, and former Minister of Science of the German Federal Republic*

DR. ADAMS.

I shall look at the questions raised by Dean Brooks purely from my own experience, which has been in two fields of science that involve considerable amounts of advanced technology. These are the field of nuclear particle physics and the field of plasma physics and nuclear fusion research.

In nuclear particle physics in particular, from the end of World War II up until around 1955, there was a very decided lead in the United States, largely due to the fact that in Europe the facilities for this research did not exist, or existed at a very low level. But from about 1960 on, because of the building of joint, common facilities in Europe at CERN, I think the United States and Europe are at about the same level.

In the case of plasma physics and fusion research, I do not think there has ever been a decided difference in progress one way or the other between the United States and Europe. However, in other fields, such as solid state physics, there was a decided lead in favor of the United States.

On the technology side, the kind of apparatus with which I have been associated is extremely large; it uses every advanced technology, and therefore it is a very good indicator of the state

33

of advanced technology in Europe. I refer to the nuclear particle accelerators, the bubble chambers, the vast data-handling systems that are used in this kind of research. To give you an order of magnitude, I think CERN has the biggest computer complex in Europe at the moment, and the machine that we are now building — a particle accelerator — is about two kilometers in diameter and costs about a billion Swiss francs.

Since CERN was set up in 1953, most of its needs have been satisfied by European industry without great difficulties. So, in general, it seems to me, the U.S. lead is really not very much. But, of course, one can point to certain technologies, as Harvey Brooks has done — to computers and solid state electronics in particular — where the purchasing has been almost always from the United States and still is today.

How did the United States gain its lead? I think the analysis Harvey Brooks gave is correct: the lead resulted from the U.S. government's interest and its massive investments in military, space, and nuclear energy projects, which provided the money and created the markets for this kind of technology. Of course, in advanced technology the cost of development increases decade by decade. For instance, it costs vastly more to develop a nuclear power station than it does to develop a fossil fuel power station. Advanced technology development costs soon exceeded the investment possibilities of private U.S. firms — even large private firms. Financing was possible only through U.S. government investment with government markets for the projects.

During this period the European investments in similar projects were relatively small. So the United States accelerated ahead of the European countries in certain of the advanced technologies. However, as we know, the rate of technological transfer was relatively high, and it was possible after a while for Europe and Japan and other countries to catch up by means of technological transfer.

Nowadays it seems that the U.S. investment in advanced technology projects is falling off, and therefore the rate of advance of U.S. development is decreasing — and decreasing to such an extent that the rate of transfer of its technology is now slightly faster than the rate of its development.

But does the U.S. lead in advanced technologies matter now? I think the answer depends largely on whether the present advanced technologies are relevant, or will be relevant, to the social needs and the new social goals which are developing in the world.

For example, if the technology required for man to go to the moon is not useful for overcoming urban congestion, transport problems, environmental pollution, the management of waste products, the exhaustion of raw materials, or any of the other problems which are now facing societies, a nation's technology may be advanced but socially irrelevant. Similarly, if this technology is no longer economically beneficial to industry for the development of products for new markets, then it is industrially and economically irrelevant.

It seems to me that we are now in a period of considerable change in social interests. These changes will ultimately be reflected in changes in government investments in new projects; there will be more emphasis on economic and social benefits to the countries. This trend in turn will affect new market development. For example, a new nonpolluting motor car or noiseless aircraft may become more socially acceptable, and therefore more salable in the future, than a motor car whose body styling changes each year, or than a supersonic jet aircraft.

Thus, instead of new products having to satisfy individual consumer demands alone, they must also satisfy communal interests. Private satisfaction will have to give way more, it seems to me, to public acceptability. This trend will affect the kinds of advanced technologies created in the future.

It seems to me that the wise countries should now be sorting out their social goals and social priorities, and wise industries should be anticipating the technologies which will prove applicable to these social goals as they emerge.

In 10 or 20 years' time, then, the advanced technologies may very well be different from those of the last 10 years, and the present ones will either be conventional technologies or just simply irrelevant. As a result, new technological gaps will emerge as, for example, one country defines the new social goals early on and starts to invest heavily in achieving these new goals. It will then accelerate ahead of the others. But through the technological transfer process the others will catch up, and the cycle will be repeated again.

I am concerned about the question of scientific knowledge. This is public knowledge, available to anybody who can use it or wants to use it. In this field, every country makes a contribution to the commonwealth of knowledge.

If a large country begins to slack off and decrease its investment in scientific research, other countries may follow. Moreover, in the future, scientific knowledge is going to be essential if we are to deal with the new problems that are coming up. Scientific knowledge up to now has been used mainly as a sort of springboard for new technologies. But it can also be important as a monitor of technology. For example, controlling pollution will require more scientific knowledge, not less of it, in the future.

Therefore, I think the world investment in basic science should go up in the future, not down. I find it very depressing to hear that the U.S. investment in science, basic science, is dropping off. Perhaps this was inevitable to a certain extent, simply because university research was so heavily funded by the government agencies covering U.S. interests in space, nuclear energy, and military developments.

In Europe I think we have a more stable system. The funding of pure research goes along with education in most European countries now, so that there is direct government funding of pure research independent of the agencies' interests. Whereas in the United States about 90% of the university research has been funded through various government agencies, and only about

36

10% directly through the government, in Europe it is almost the other way around.

LORD BOWDEN.

With many of Dr. Adams' observations I find myself very profoundly in agreement. In particular, I like his point that the problems of science are dramatically changing, and although it may well be that some branches of science have been worked out, the problems that remain are far more complicated than those we have solved. Unless some of these new problems can be solved, the whole world will be at risk.

We are wholly dependent on science and technology to survive in our present form of society. Unless a great deal more fundamental science is applied to the problems which have arisen because of our very successes, we shall collapse. Arguments based on the assumption that scientific problems are disappearing are, in my view, totally without foundation.

The story we heard this morning from Dr. Brooks is astonishingly like many speeches which were made about a hundred years ago. There was a time when the industrial and scientific dominance of England in the world was far greater than anything that America has achieved in the last couple of decades. Lancashire used to boast that it clothed England in the first shift before breakfast on a Monday morning, and clothed the world in the rest of the week. The dominance of the textile trade in Lancashire over the whole world market was complete.

The decline in the state of English manufacturing from 1851, when we had our great Exhibition, to 1861, when there was another Exhibition, was far more dramatic, far more total, and far more sudden than anything that has occurred in America in the past few years. The reason was perfectly simple: *no* country can expect indefinitely to monopolize an industry, a science, or anything else, and *all* countries in the Western world are in many ways capable of doing the same sort of thing in their own time.

37

So the first point I want to make is that this story of a sudden decline in American dominance was inevitable in view of the fact that no country can indefinitely perpetuate a position of dominance.

The second point I want to make is that arguments about, for example, the lack of interest of professors in their students, and their leaving too much teaching to unskilled graduates of arts, are not new. This very same complaint led to major riots in the University of Paris in the year 1606 which were even worse than those in 1968. I do not think we should be surprised that such riots are happening again. They are, as it were, inherent in the nature of the university machine.

Next, I want to come to the particular problems of America. The first is the extraordinary problem which flows in any country from a long-continued exponential growth. In fact, I believe that there have been 341,000 Ph.D. degrees awarded in America since the first ones were given at Yale University about 80 years ago, and half of them have been given in the last 8 years. The population explosion among Ph.D.s corresponds to a doubling of the population about every 5 or 6 years. It is evident that if this growth were to go on much longer, every American would be a Ph.D. and so would be those few draft animals that survive on the American farms.

Now, the growth rate of expenditure on science in many countries, very surprisingly, was about 16% compounded for a period of about 40 years — from the beginning of the 1930's or perhaps the late 1920's until the middle, let us say, of the last decade. That growth rate applied in England, Germany, and Russia as well as the United States.

Now, no country had a gross national product rising at anything like that 16% rate. And it is perfectly evident that no government can permit so great a disparity in the cost of science, the numbers of Ph.D.s, and the growth of the rest of the economy. In England we realized this five or six years ago — I was myself concerned with these things — and we decided that the rate of growth had to be cut down to a relatively slow and steady rate so there would not be a catastrophic change when it was suddenly cut back, because our question was not *whether* it would be cut back, but *when* it would be cut back.

The difference, in very round and simple terms, between our policy in England and the American policy was that we realized in time the rate would have to go down, and so we cut it deliberately; the Americans believed that 16% was the number God had always intended and stuck with it until it was reduced very suddenly a few years ago.

A sharp drop in growth rate inevitably causes chaos in any system of education because the whole structure of a university is geared to the rate at which the system as a whole is expanding. The size of the graduate school depends on this, and the graduates teach the undergraduates; the whole thing is systematized so as to adjust itself to a particular assumed rate of growth.

I talked to some American university presidents who told me about a university that is unlikely to recruit another Ph.D. physicist for 20 years. This is because it has so many physicists as a result of earlier recruiting. So now all these faculty scientists are going to grow old together. This will undoubtedly destroy that physics department. Such is the consequence of an abrupt, sudden discontinuity in the rate of growth.

I think that much of the Americans' discontent is due to the suddenness with which an inevitable change has afflicted them. How they are going to get over it? I do not know. I do know that this slowdown was bound to have come about before very long, and that it would have been less disconcerting had it happened rather more slowly.

After all, exponential growth has occurred many times before. The Abbey of Cluny was founded in the year 941 A.D. For the next 250 years abbeys were founded all over Europe, and each of them tried to found others in its own image. Now, this is a recipe for exponential growth. Two hundred years after Cluny was founded, there were over 7,500 abbeys of various sorts in Europe. Had this same rate of growth continued for another hundred years, I believe any statistician could show that every adult European male would have been a monk. I will not presume to say what this would have done to the population explosion at the time!

The preeminence of the United States in pure science during the 1950's came not, I suspect, from the intrinsic merit of the American population, but from the fact that American universities bought with gold many of the best scientists in Europe. Before World War II, according to Vannevar Bush, Europe had supplied the pure research upon which America traditionally depended. This role would never have been reversed had it not been for the devastation caused by the war. America took such an enormous number of the ablest scientists, particularly from Germany, that her immense scientific growth was inevitable for that reason alone.

I believe myself that Sir William Bragg had a very fundamental point when he said that throughout the world we get one good physicist per annum for every million of the population. He thought this ratio was, roughly speaking, independent of race and origin. Therefore, once the economic situation changes so that science can in fact be done properly, there is a strong probability that Chinese science will be the best in the world, if only because there are more Chinese than there are English or Americans.

I believe that much of what the Americans are worried about is, first of all, the fact that they cannot expect to sustain in the 1970's an impetus they got in the 1930's and 1940's because of the influx of some of the ablest men in Europe. Their immense national skills in producing technology are exactly analogous to those which we once showed in England and which other countries in Europe have in turn shown. It is now time for the rest of the world to redress the balance which was artificially distorted by historical circumstances.

Dean Brooks talked about unemployment among graduates

40

and the slump in the advanced technological industries. This is a phenomenon which is worrying everyone in Europe. I can speak more particularly for my own country. In England we are suffering from a lack of employment opportunities for Ph.D. chemists, for Ph.D. physicists, and, in fact, for graduates as a whole. I have talked to the graduate employment offices of the great English firms, and I find that, for example, ICI, which used to employ about 600 new graduates every year, expected at the beginning of this year to cut down its recruitment to 240, and in fact recruited only 110.

I find to my horror that some of the great firms of accountants, like Peat Marwick and Price Waterhouse, are *each* recruiting this year more graduates than the whole of ICI. So when British industry does collapse, we shall at least know the whole of the financial details in the process! For the problem of the slump in advanced technological industries is *not* confined to the United States, and graduate unemployment is *not* confined to the United States. We have developed the same problems ourselves — on a scale which is not very different. A recession is exported quickly where there is dependence on advanced technology, and if it starts in America, it spreads extremely rapidly to the rest of the world.

PROFESSOR COLOMBO.

First, let me say that I agree with Dean Brooks's general views concerning the scientific and technological relationship between the United States and Europe.

It is important to "demystify" the concept of the technology gap and to try to understand in depth the complex problems that determine the present patterns of scientific and technological performance in various countries. I agree that a distinction should be made between advanced technology and general technology. While the former is important in certain key sectors of industrial activity, the latter is related to the overall productivity pattern of the industrial sector as a whole.

41

As far as advanced technology is concerned, it should be recognized that in Europe nationalist spirit has jeopardized international efforts such as Euratom and has made impossible the technological cooperation needed to enable Europe to compete in the advanced technology markets. The failure of most cooperative European R&D efforts is due to the fact that up to now there has been no coherent European R&D policy, not even a body capable of defining such policy and of putting it into action.

Therefore, we are faced with an absurd situation in which individual states pursue rival programs in many scientific and technological fields. Yet there is general agreement that the resources and efforts of individual European countries are inadequate in various fields of advanced technology. Under these circumstances, it is clear that the problem is mostly of a political nature, and that only by an honest reappraisal of the common objectives in the light of a wider and stronger European community will it be possible to establish the scientific and technological cooperation needed for a European take-off in advanced technology.

As far as general technology is concerned, I do not believe that there is any substantial gap between the United States and Europe. This is due to several factors, including the fact that in Europe, as Dean Brooks said, R&D effort has not been diverted away from civilian industries as much as it has in the United States.

In recent years the liberalization of trade within the European Economic Community has created in Europe an integrated market of a size comparable to that of the United States. This has induced a process of structural modification within the industrial sector where, through acquisitions, mergers, and the like, European firms are achieving an adequate size. The full effects of such a concentration process, which will continue and will involve more and more transnational concentrations, are yet to be seen. This process will, of course, have a bearing on the reorientation of industrial research in Europe and could be beneficial in improving communications between industry and universities.

Thus, there are good hopes for a continued productivity increase in Europe as a result of technological change. But I also believe there is still an ample potential for increasing productivity, due to a considerable reservoir of scientific manpower. On the other hand, any further productivity increase in U.S. industry will have to come from real progress in technology and the application of scientific knowledge, without any substantial input of additional manpower.

The recent study by the Organisation for Economic Cooperation and Development (OECD) Secretary General's ad hoc group on science policy, chaired by Dean Brooks, has clearly shown that there is an urgent need for the elaboration of a new type of science policy, designed to master economic growth, balancing quantity with quality. Similar conclusions were drawn by the National Goals Research Staff appointed by the President of the United States. The need for a balanced growth aimed at improving the so-called "quality of life" is particularly relevant to the affluent society, where the present mix of science and technology reflects an emphasis on achieving economic growth. The social costs of economic growth in an affluent society have generated a public concern that has not yet crystallized in clear science and technology objectives. Parallel with this concern and discontent, one can observe a growing inefficiency of the system that is due to the progressive loss of motivation on the part of employees even at intermediate and executive levels, and perhaps to the lack of valid incentives.

Obviously, we need a better understanding of the technological, economic, and social phenomena. At the same time, it appears that the conventional tools of economic science are no longer sufficient to cope with the needs of society, and that traditional market mechanisms are no longer adequate.

The steps needed to overcome the problem are not yet exactly known, but it is likely that the ground rules of the market economy should be changed, keeping in mind the evolving social objectives. It seems to me that Europe, with its diversified experience in national planning and in governmental action toward social goals, could play an extremely important role in the achievement of a balanced, harmonious development of society. In this effort, Europe will no doubt be helped by a more humanistic and more complex culture than the United States has. The cultural problem is probably the most important single factor for future progress. In what ways is it important?

First, culture affects the problem of building a constructive relationship between (1) governments and political power in general, and (2) industrial enterprises, be they nationally based or multinational. It is not so much a matter of conflict between these forces, not so much a matter of controlling technology within political systems while retaining competition, as it is a matter of achieving a deep understanding of the global goals of society and of the ways and means to reach these goals. It is a matter of understanding that political and industrial powers must conquer together. This understanding process, in my opinion, cannot develop unless men of culture, including humanists and scientists, play the kind of role they played, for example, in eighteenth-century Europe.

Second, culture affects relations with the developing countries. If we want, as we should, to contribute to the progress of such countries, we must first of all recognize that their needs in terms of science and technology are quite different from those of developed countries. The differences stem not only from the very condition of underdevelopment, but also indeed from differences in philosophy, tradition, and culture. It is absolutely essential to harmonize economic development with such cultural values in order to avoid major strains and, perhaps, a disaster.

Summing up, I feel, as Dean Brooks does, that the circumstances that placed the United States in the lead in science and technology have gradually changed and are still changing. Considering the problem from a European angle, I believe that the question of advanced technologies has a political connotation;

much will depend on the will to establish common European objectives. As far as general technology is concerned, I believe that Europe will play a major role in connection with the problems of advanced as well as developing societies. This is the challenge for the younger European generations.

DR. STOLTENBERG.

I, too, agree with Dean Brooks's theme. The United States is experiencing some new problems and trends only a few years earlier than other industrial societies will. In this respect the Americans are frontrunners again, but for a shorter time. Many American problems are known already to European societies, governments, and scientists. The new tangents and controversial discussions of priorities, goals, and social implications in the United States create an experience which will have a strong influence on the European scene.

During the 1950's and 1960's Europe adopted many elements of the American structure in scientific and technological programs, though on a smaller scale. We gained many achievements from the American experience. I think we also copied some U.S. mistakes concerning priorities. I refer especially to our problems and failures in the aerospace industry.

I want to support the position of Dean Brooks on another point. We must avoid the exaggerations of the past. Only a few years ago the European debates referred to the increasing technological gap in all relevant fields. This concept was forcefully presented to European public opinion by writers, politicians, and many others; they had a strong influence and sometimes a misleading influence. On the other hand, I think these exaggerations had some value because they showed Europeans the problem, the task, and the difficulties.

Now we have to avoid new exaggerations in the opposite direction. This danger may be more present in the United States than in Europe at the moment, but the distrust, the disappointment, the skepticism about the results of modern science and technology are becoming more and more a basic European problem. When we look into the results of empirical social research concerning the attitudes of the 20- to 25-year-olds in Europe, we see evidence of this trend.

There may be one advantage on the European side: a more balanced structure of R&D expenditures between government and industry. For instance, in the Federal Republic of Germany more than 50% of the national R&D budget comes from nongovernmental sources. In past discussions this seemed to be a failure of the government, but it may be an advantage under the conditions elaborated by Dean Brooks, because it reflects the smaller role of military, aerospace, and nuclear projects in the overall national science and research program. Also, it reflects a greater emphasis on the problems of application, which are very key problems now.

We have other European countries — for example, Switzerland — with very successful technological and industrial development efforts. The public expenditures may be less than 20%. But, on the other hand, I think that most advantages are still on the side of the United States. These advantages are its higher gross national product, its still far higher expenditure for science and technology compared with Western Europe, and its great national market of 200 million people.

You will remember that a European Professor, H.B.G. Casimir, some years ago referred to the technological gap by saying that its closing could be very easily achieved by separating the 50 states of the United States into individual units with trade barriers, different corporate laws, and independent national tax legislation. This suggests our structural disadvantage compared with the United States.

But our *real* failure is that while we have had a Common Market for 14 years, and while we have in the Treaties of Rome the goals of common regulations in all relevant fields, we have no common science and development policy for Western Europe. Undoubtedly some single projects of cooperation, especially in

46

basic research, have proved very successful — for example, CERN and ESRO. And in some fields of basic and applied research we have a lead. But many of our efforts are very disappointing.

When we look for the reason for failure, we find it is not so much a lack of capacity of the scientists and technicians as the impossibility of gaining a really effective organization without a political structure. This need is one of the unsolved tasks of Europe.

Equally important is our failure to establish the basic conditions for multinational industrial development in Western Europe. We have, as I mentioned before, no common corporate law; and we have no common taxation policy. These are extreme barriers which must be surmounted in order to achieve the industrial and commercial goals of the Common Market, and to develop a European multinational society that can maintain the necessary actual and future expenditures for science and technology.

What about European technology at less advanced levels? Less sophisticated production is, to a great extent, emigrating away from Western Europe to other countries. For example, camera production and the optical industry are going from Germany to Singapore, Taiwan, and such less-developed Western European nations as Ireland and Portugal. This trend may increase in the future as we experience fast-rising costs and inflation. Here is a great danger for Germany and other Western European countries. It makes it more important for us to keep up with the most advanced technological developments because of their significance to the economic future.

Finally, there is the question of the free international exchange of ideas, results of research, goods, and currencies for mutual progress in the Western world. When we compare our situation, with its achievements and failures, with that of Eastern Europe, I think we realize that the restrictions of exchange, publication, and ideas which exist there are some of the reasons that the so-called Socialist countries cannot keep pace with the Western world, especially in applications of technology. But this could change. So I would advise that we look very carefully to their plans and achievements, for they could become stronger competitors in many technological fields than they have been in the past.

We must accept the fact that the interaction between scientific expenditure and progress, on the one side, and commercial success, on the other, is not so simple as we once believed. I understand it is irritating for our American friends to realize that they spent the most money on science in the 1950's and 1960's, yet they now have real economic troubles. Some of the simple formulas for progress that we all used did not prove to be right. We have to try to clarify the conditions of interaction in a more sophisticated way. I personally believe that this need could be a new area of European and U.S. cooperation in the future.

Following the remarks of Dr. Stoltenberg, Lord Zuckerman opened the discussion to members of the audience. Parts of the ensuing dialogue are reproduced here.

PHILIPPE HEYMANN (VISION MAGAZINE).
My question is for Dean Brooks, but in fact I disagree a bit with some of the talks by Professor Colombo and Dr. Stoltenberg.

I wonder if the barriers in Europe are not in fact a pretext for business for not acting or doing things. I know, from trying to establish a European magazine, that there are a lot of barriers and frontiers. But I wonder if in fact there is not in the United States a kind of capacity to adapt to new situations, to new challenges, and to new problems which means that the gap is not going to decrease, and that in two or three years the United States will open it up again.

In fact, even when Dr. Colombo speaks about the possibility for Europe to play a big role in social and cultural fields, I wonder if in those fields too the United States is not going to show us the way. Some big American firms like Texas Instruments are preparing projects that will produce a kind of social revolution.

DEAN BROOKS.

This is a hard question to answer. It certainly is true that there is a tremendous amount of adaptation going on in the U.S. system which is not very visible yet; it takes this sort of thing a good deal of time to germinate, because of time needed to redeploy resources, and so on. So there may be something in what you say — that a new kind of gap will develop. Actually, though, I think that this is not so likely because of the complexity of the new priorities. I don't think you are going to see the suddenness of change that you did with respect, for example, to the take-off of the U.S. space program in the late 1950's.

It is true that one of the advantages that the United States might have in this area is the much greater relative strength of its social sciences. In many respects European countries have been more successful in the application of the social sciences than the United States has, but it enjoys a tremendous *base* of knowledge and capability that it could draw on.

MR. HAWRYLYSHYN.

I have been very much intrigued by the proposition of Dr. Adams. Therefore, let me raise an issue. One could hypothesize that human society excels in things that it considers very important, and therefore focuses its vital energy on the accomplishment of such objectives. In the United States economic success has clearly been considered important; on the value scale it really has been very close to the top. Technological progress has seemed to be an instrument for succeeding in that objective. Therefore, the country has succeeded in technological programs

49

because they have been a factor in accomplishing its priority objective.

Now, if economic success is no longer seen as being so important or so relevant, and if the value system as such is changing, then I would imagine the United States could regain the technological lead only if such a lead is seen as important in acquiring greater social and political wisdom and a happier, more balanced society. But somehow I am not terribly sure that technology will be seen that way.

DR. ADAMS.

Most of these social problems that are coming out are really a question of survival, which, of course, is a very strong force indeed. It is this that leads me to believe that the economic benefit will be modified by social benefit in the future. If it were only a question of wanting to live happier or better in some way, I think you might be right, but many of the problems I mentioned that are coming up now are problems of survival, and most countries react pretty strongly in those circumstances.

LORD BOWDEN.

I believe that the Americans' greatest strength, in a curious sort of way, is to be found in the original Morrill Act of 1861, which in effect founded a series of universities in which it was held to be respectable and intellectually responsible to study any problem at all which was a concern of society. This came at a time when classical education dominated the universities of England and, to a degree, of the Continent, and when it was held to be quite impossible to study practical problems like agriculture anywhere. But America did it.

Their great strength in developing their universities was derived from that Act. In a sense, it is this very tradition which is in the process of destroying them, because the interests of society have become equated temporarily with the interests of the Pentagon. That is why the American universities have ac-

50

cepted pressures imposed upon them by the Pentagon to take defense work; the work is seen as necessary to the interests of the United States.

In the future this public interest tradition will again make it possible for the Americans to study problems not academically respectable, such as how to solve problems of contamination, and how to organize large groups of people living in cities.

I am sure that the Americans' tradition, if they can accept it for what it is, would be their greatest single source of strength. What I fear is that they will come — as we English once did with the classics — to regard the total field of respectable knowledge as already having been circumscribed. It was a Dean of Christ Church in the 1860's who remarked in a university sermon at Oxford that "The advantages of a classical education are twofold: it allows us to look with contempt upon those who have not shared it, and it fits in the places of emolument both in this world and that which is to come."

Now, this seems to resemble the view of too many scientists. They regard themselves as having a virtual monopoly on intellectual respectability, they tend to despise people who have not been similarly trained, and they are quite sure of their places of emolument in this world, and perhaps in the next. It is this sort of attitude which is growing up in the States, as it grew up in England a hundred years ago, which is dangerous.

LORD ZUCKERMAN.

I am now going to call upon Dean Harvey Brooks for five more minutes in which he can pull out from the discussion certain points and comment on them.

DEAN BROOKS.

Lord Bowden mentioned the abrupt turnaround in the U.S. situation. I think this was almost inevitable. He pointed to the U.S. system of support of universities. As I mentioned in my talk, the whole growth of federal support of science in the universities arose purely as a by-product of other social decisions. There was never any government *policy* for the support of universities.

I would point out that the Pentagon was really very much less of an influence than the medical research complex was. At the present time the amount of money from the Defense Department going into university research is only about 10% of the total, and the highest it ever reached was 18% to 20% (although the figure was somewhat higher in the physical sciences).

There is very little federal leverage on the university system with respect to its size, expansion, or contraction. Control is effected in a decentralized way through competition between many small units — the states and even the municipalities — and competitive pressures therefore have tended to continue an expansion long after it has been justified by the totality of circumstances. This certainly is one of our problems.

I very much agree with Lord Bowden's remarks regarding the Morrill Act and its influence on the general approach to universities' functions. But I am not as pessimistic as he is about the universities in the United States circumscribing the areas of respectable knowledge, as the European and British universities did, because I can already see considerable countervailing trends in that direction.

There is a point to be made about the Morrill Act. I refer to the great success story of agricultural research, which grew up in the university system in the United States. I think few people realize that it has been a success only in the last 20 to 25 years. The tremendous growth of agricultural productivity in the agricultural sector in the United States is a relatively recent phenomenon. The whole system of agricultural research and extension, and the coordinate industry that grew up around it, are more recent history than sometimes appears from the various writings.

I think this illustrates the problem with which we are going to be faced in the future. That is, it takes a long time for a new technical structure to crystallize around new social priorities. You can argue, in fact, that it took nearly a century for the successful system of agricultural innovation to crystallize around the new social priorities symbolized by the Morrill Act. It took many years for the military-industrial complex to crystallize around the new military priorities that arose in the Cold War. It may take similar periods of time for a successful system of innovation to crystallize around the new priorities represented by the quality of life and other needs that we have been talking about.

LORD ZUCKERMAN.

Dean Brooks has both posed and answered the question, "Have the circumstances that placed the United States in the lead in science and technology changed?" Circumstances *have* changed. The position of the United States *has* changed. But equally, I think, the discussion has revealed the fact that the problems of the United States are not unique.

Lord Bowden has suggested that we are moving into a phase in which all of these problems are going to be common problems. He referred to the possibilities of international research; undoubtedly, there is scientific unemployment in countries other than the United States; and there is far too little investment in technology in all our countries.

I agree with Dr. Stoltenberg that the high-technology industries remain very relevant. He reminded us of developments that are taking place in other parts of the world. He referred in particular to Eastern Europe. We must not forget that high-technology industries are going ahead there as well. And they are relevant to very many fields, including fields of low technology.

When we talk about productivity, I don't know whether the problems we are dealing with are really technological problems. At the present moment, there are a million or so people unemployed in the United Kingdom. Is it high-technology industry we want, new investment, or what? Are we dealing with factors other than purely technological ones when we consider the

53

reasons for low productivity? Those matters have not been touched on.

What is clear from the discussion is that society is taking a different view of its priorities.

Dr. Adams referred to irrelevant and relevant technologies. The relevant technologies were those which will be called into being in order to deal with environmental, population, and other social problems. We must remember that none of these technologies is going to be brought into being if there is a lack of continued economic growth. If the time lag between the crystallization of the new technologies is as long as it is likely to be, we are going to need industrial production from existing technologies, profit, new resources. Otherwise, our present social problems are not going to be dealt with and the quality of life will not be improved. The wealth of the world must continue to increase while we improve the quality of life.

In effect, what we are talking about is the problem of bringing into the costs of production all the factors which affect such costs, including external or social costs, which until now have not really been taken into account. A society can live with the ill effects of technology as long as it wants to do so. But one day it can decide to do so no longer. This was what happened when child labor was abolished. Factory acts to improve safety came about in spite of the fact that they added to costs of production. All such external costs can be dealt with if society wants. But they will be dealt with at a cost.

I believe that calculations have been made in the United States which indicate that to deal with the ecological devastation of the past and to prevent continuing pollution of the environment will necessitate something like 2% of the gross national product for some years to come. This amount cannot be diverted immediately to the task. Calculations have been made in the United Kingdom, too; here the figure is not quite so high.

I understand that recent U.S. legislation has, in effect, added over the next five years something like $20 billion a year in economic costs because of environmental needs. That figure happens to be slightly greater than the total volume of all aid to the underdeveloped countries at the present moment.

We have got to get our social priorities right. Our social priorities are international priorities. The world is not going to continue at peace, whatever happens to the advanced countries, if the underdeveloped countries go on as they are at the present moment. Indeed, as we know from the tragic cases of India and Pakistan, it is too easy for social problems to spill over into major political problems which cannot be contained in a peaceful framework.

I think there *is* going to be more international cooperation. Professor Colombo and Dr. Stoltenberg have referred to the major changes that have been taking place in Europe during the past few years. The European Economic Community is a step in the right direction. Admittedly, it still is not what one would like it to be. The political structure of Europe is not the best that could be devised in order to take full advantage of what science and technology have done, and can do, for the benefit of mankind.

It is going to take time, I suppose, for the matters referred to by Dr. Stoltenberg to be corrected. But let us hope that eventually the political structure of Europe will be such that we *can* share the burden of looking after the future in suitable ways.

International cooperation is going to be called for on a far wider scale than just the Common Market — of that I am quite certain. To develop new technologies will take much time, and during that time let us not throw out the baby with the bath water, as we are now in danger of doing. Otherwise there is not going to be the economic growth or resources to correct the problems. There will then be no chance that we or the next generation will get our social priorities right.

3

Closing the Technology Gap— The Japanese Approach

By SOHEI NAKAYAMA

President, Overseas Technical Cooperation Agency of Japan, formerly Chairman of the Industrial Bank of Japan

In an effort to shed some light on the far-reaching implications of the theme of this conference, I should like to discuss four different but interrelated aspects of technology in Japan: first, the role of technological innovation in economic growth; second, various factors that made rapid technological innovation possible; third, the pattern of technological development and the unique features of technology developed in Japan; and, finally, the development of technology in the future.

It was a decade and a half ago — that is, in the mid-1950's — that Japan began to undertake technological innovation in earnest. Among the manifold economic and social conditions that served to promote technological innovation in our country, three, in my opinion, were particularly important.

First, about that time Japan had accomplished the preliminary task of building an economic foundation firm enough to allow technological innovation. To elaborate on this point, Japan, having been totally destroyed in the process of World War II, had to exert her utmost efforts and give priority to the rehabilitation and repair of destroyed and damaged production facilities in order to try to restore living standards to the pre-war level, since the people were in a miserable condition as a result of our defeat. By 1955, about ten years after the termination of the war, Japan had eventually succeeded, through back-breaking efforts, in restoring the pre-war level both in living standards and in industrial activity, thereby building the economic strength upon which further progress could realistically be made.

A second condition which fostered technological innovation was the change that had taken place in the international political and economic environment surrounding the Japanese economy. Having lost overseas territories as a consequence of defeat in war, Japan had to depend on imports for most of her basic production factors, such as energy and other natural resources.

In the post-war recovery period, Japan acquired a substantial portion of the necessary foreign exchange from U.S. aid and from special procurements arising out of the Korean War. But eventually it became imperative to enhance exports on a "fair competition" basis so that the Japanese economy could create the preconditions for autonomous economic growth and move beyond the stage of dependence. Even though the Japanese economy had regained the economic level of pre-war days, there was still a wide gap between the then-advanced nations and Japan. Japan was far behind the great strides in technological innovation that had been made in the West, mainly in the United States, during and after the war.

Without a concentrated endeavor to close this gap, Japan's self-reliant economic development, with exports as the axis, would not have been possible.

Third, I would like to draw your attention to the change in the values and life style of the Japanese people that has accompanied technological progress. The post-war social influences represented by the Occupation Forces stationed in Japan or by the flood of American movies brought a sweeping change to the pre-war way of life, where emphasis formerly had been put on simplicity and frugality. The comic strip named "Blondie," by Chic Young, firmly engraved upon the minds of the Japanese men the convenience of electric refrigerators, where bottles of Coke and thick sandwiches could be kept. The Japanese housewife was also quick to note how much free time Blondie had as a result of being able to do her household work efficiently with electrical appliances, such as the automatic washing machine and handy vacuum cleaner.

The demand for durable consumer goods, the ownership of which had substantially spread in Western countries as early as the 1930's, awoke in Japan between the end of the war and the mid-1950's. It can be said that in this manner the way had been paved for a full-fledged mass consumption society pursuant to the rapid development of the Americanization, if you will, among the Japanese people. Under these economic and social conditions unique to Japan which I have described, the technological innovation of our country proceeded very extensively and quite rapidly, in a manner considerably different from that of Western countries.

On the one hand, Japanese technological innovation aimed at the enhancement of competitiveness in exports and rapidly progressed in the field of electronics, the marco-molecule chemical industry, and techniques of large-scale automation. And, on the other hand, parallel to this advance in new and high-grade technology, our production technology of durable consumer goods, which in Western nations had already matured before the war, made headway in the area of passenger cars and household electrical appliances, such as refrigerators and vacuum cleaners, in response to the active demand for those goods stimulated by the change in the Japanese people's life style and sense of values.

Needless to say, the development of these two types of technology did not advance independently of each other. For instance, plastics, a product of the macro-molecule chemical industry, came to be used for improving the quality and performance of durable consumer goods; and the techniques of large-scale automation were applied to cut down the price, standardize the quality, and achieve the mass production of these goods.

In short, the special characteristic of the Japanese technological innovation is that "delayed" and "advanced" innovations started simultaneously and developed rapidly, interacting with each other.

This twofold nature of technological innovation gave scope and breadth to our progress in Japan and was instrumental in establishing the high rate of growth of the Japanese economy after the mid-1950's. The technological innovation aimed at automating and enlarging the scale of production not only stimulated new equipment investment in manufacturing industries, but also multiplied investment in capital goods industries as a whole. In addition, the successive debut of new merchandise such as nylons and electric refrigerators and washing machines, supported by a vigorous demand, helped to amplify the mechanism of spiral expansion of investment.

The primary element that has constantly sustained Japan's enjoyment of an annual real growth rate of over 10% on the average for the past 15 years is the aforementioned extensive technological innovation, without which the Japanese economy would not have been able to develop to what it is today. According to our estimate, technological innovation accounted directly for 40% of the economic growth during this period. If the multiplier effect of such innovation were taken into consideration, the rate would be much larger.

All in all, the great economic growth of Japan would have been impossible without explosive technological innovation. The next question is: What are the factors that made this explosion possible?

It would have been impossible for such extensive and rapid technological innovation to occur entirely through self-developed technology. Thus, had Japan adopted the policy of carrying out technological innovation by means of domestically developed techniques only, its speed would have been much slower and its scope much narrower. As we look back, Japan's technological innovation appears to have gained its impetus mainly from advanced foreign technology.

It can be said, therefore, that technological innovation in our country owes its success to, among other things, the favorable international environment that made it possible for Japan to introduce foreign technology. However, it was not only Japan that was endowed with this favorable international environment. As a next step, therefore, I would like to examine the reasons why Japan has succeeded on such a unique scale.

Unusual Capacities

There seem to be roughly three reasons: first, Japan's ability to absorb foreign technology; second, its economic base, which allowed such an introduction; and third, Japan's system for promoting technology introduction.

We should look at the first reason, Japan's ability to absorb foreign technology, from two different angles. One is what we might call the macro-dimension of ability, as represented by the total level of Japan's technology around the mid-1950's, when technological innovation was about to accelerate. The other is the micro-dimension of ability — the way of thinking about foreign technology or the ability to digest it. To put the conclusion first, the great success of technological innovation in Japan owes much to the good soil that exists in both the macro and the micro dimensions.

The first step toward industrialization was taken in our country in the latter half of the nineteenth century. The new government established the Constitutional Monarchy under the Emperor, superseding the feudalistic military government which had been in power for centuries. The new government embarked upon the modernization of industries for the purpose of bringing wealth and military strength to Japan. The result of this effort was that, by the Second World War, Japan had succeeded in accumulating technological capacity comparable to that of highly industrialized countries in a wide range of industrial fields, from cotton spinning, steel, and shipbuilding, to aircraft. Of course, it cannot be denied that, since the national goal up to the time of the war was the building of military strength, technological development had been geared to defense-related technology. However, through the elevation of the technological level in the military field, the overall level of technology had been considerably upgraded as well.

It is true that there was a wide technological gap between Japan and the West because, for 15 years after the start of the war, Japan was in the midst of destruction and reconstruction and was too busy to concentrate on technological development. But with the high level of technology accumulated before the war, it was not too difficult for Japan to close the then-existing gap.

To cite an example, the birth of the modern shipbuilding industry in Japan dates back merely a century. By around the turn of the nineteenth century — and only 30 years after its birth — the industry had the expertise to build a cruiser of 20,000 tons, which was regarded as gigantic at the time. From then on, the industry built one mammoth ship after another, making Japan a leading naval power. This was the result of great efforts to absorb and improve Western technology by marshaling abundant funds and human resources to attain a powerful navy. The shipbuilding technology in Japan, though centering around battleship building, had developed to such an extent that it surpassed the international level. It says much for Japan's pre-war accumulation of technology that Japanese industry could not only master the welding method and the block construction system devised right after the war, but could go so far as to develop the one-side automatic welding method and the afloat welding method.

Next I should like to consider Japan's micro-dimensional ability, the capacity to absorb technology. With regard to this, there are two elements: one is the inborn national disposition, and the other, the ability to understand and digest a new technology.

In regard to the inborn national disposition, attention should be given to the flexibility of the Japanese. Psychologically, they do not tend to refuse things foreign — whether in the field of culture or in technology — and once they become aware that it is worth the effort, they will adopt new things, even at the sacrifice of conventional methods or ways of thinking.

The phrase used to be popular among Japanese that, after World War II, women and stockings became stronger and fathers weaker. This expresses with a touch of cynicism the drastic change that Japan experienced after the war. In the pre-war days, due to the history of feudalistic military government, the status of women was low and the authority of fathers was ex-

64

tremely great. This way of thinking was discarded and the equality of the sexes was advocated, as democracy — which prizes equality of individuals — was introduced during the Occupation period in place of the authoritarian philosophy prevalent before the war. I might add that nylon stockings, brought to the Japanese market after the war, became the idol of women, and in a very short span of time spread throughout the country, driving silk stockings from the market.

We Japanese realize that this kind of disposition is one of our national shortcomings, in the sense that it reflects a lack of individuality; but, at the same time, we think that this free and flexible attitude toward things foreign greatly assisted our country in settling foreign technology on the Japanese soil so smoothly and rapidly.

The excellent ability of the Japanese to understand and digest new technology can be attributed to the pre-war accumulation of technology already mentioned. But, more fundamentally, it is the natural outcome of the high educational level: attendance at elementary schools and junior high schools has been nearly 100% since long before the war, and the percentage of students entering higher institutions of learning is now 80% at high school level and 25% at university level. This has enabled industries to obtain manpower to shoulder new technology. However, we must bear in mind that the absorption and digestion of foreign technology so far described would not have flourished without a background of adequate economic conditions.

Post-war Japan went through a drastic institutional change as a result of various measures broadly termed "economic democratization." The land reform and the number of institutions for protection of the rights of laborers contributed to the domestic market, which had until that time remained very limited, and presented for the new mechandise born of new technologies a stable and large domestic market consisting of 100 million people.

Moreover, with the dissolution of the *Zaibatsu* — Mitsui,

Mitsubishi, and Sumitomo — which had controlled the economy before the war, the oligopolistic structure of our economy was transformed into a structure of free competition. Divided, each enterprise was driven to modernize its plant and equipment and develop new products if it expected to compete and survive.

The streamlining of the environment of domestic demand and the introduction of keen competition for survival served as a stimulus to import and master more advanced technologies and to develop new and native technology upon the foundation of imported know-how.

Now I will consider the third factor responsible for Japan's success in technological innovation, its system for promoting technological innovation.

In the first place, through the dissolution of the *Zaibatsu,* the separation of ownership from management became more drastic than in the West. And, as a result, young and flexible executives, equipped with professional knowledge, emerged in large number. Some of them had formerly had professional training in technical fields, and they were keen on accelerating the growth of their enterprises by introducing new technology and taking advantage of the hidden but potential demand evolving in the market. It was not unusual for the president himself to lead a project team for the development of new products.

To give you an example, the former president of the Sony Corporation, Mr. Ibuka, said once, about his own experience in successfully developing an epoch-making color TV set using the trinitron system:

"The unique feature in the process of the development of trinitron TV sets is that the top management has participated in the project from the predevelopment stage. This enabled the top management to make quick decisions and to strategically allocate personnel, space, and budget. Moreover, in proceeding with the development program we could eliminate unnecessary processes, thus raising efficiency."

In addition to this system of combining and integrating management and technology, extensive study and training programs, including the dispatch of personnel to overseas institutions, have been conducted effectively, thanks to the stable labor relations created by the life-time employment system. These factors also should properly be evaluated for their contribution to the advancement of technological innovation.

In crediting this good management system favorable to the acceleration of technological innovation, we must not forget the important function which the government has played.

The Economic Planning Agency, which makes plans regarding the administration of the Japanese economy, emphasized in its 1956 "White Paper" the importance of technological innovation. And ever since then, despite the scarce foreign-exchange reserves, the government has adopted the policy of permitting the introduction of foreign technology by private enterprises.

These have been the reasons why technological innovation has been able to advance in our country. What, then, has been the concrete process of innovation, and how should we evaluate the present level of technology?

Anatomy of Innovation

As I have stated already, technological innovation in Japan owes a great deal of its start to the induction of foreign technology. Foreign know-how and native technology have produced two technological patterns.

The development of technology in such industries as petrochemicals, synthetic fibers, and electronics, which were newly established after World War II, has continued to depend entirely on foreign know-how. This kind of technology can be called the "foreign-technology dependent" type. On the other hand, in the industrial sectors which had a rather extensive accumulation of native know-how before the war, such as shipbuilding, steel, optical instruments, clock making, and automobiles, foreign know-how has been introduced in order to enhance native techniques heretofore in use. This kind of innovation may be called the "combination of domestic and foreign technology" type.

Technological innovation in Japan, having taken these two patterns from the start, continued in this way after the war. In the late 1950's and early 1960's, foreign technology was absorbed, but thenceforth it gradually became possible for Japanese industry to accelerate innovation by its own know-how and also to produce new products by using the self-innovated technology. For instance, in the field of electronics, new products, such as the transistorized radio and television, the desk-top computer, and so forth, have been brought forth to the market one after another; and in the steel industry, blast-furnace techniques have been developed to the extent of being exported overseas.

The amount of Japanese technology exported abroad cannot be said to be at a high level today, but since 1962 or 1963 there has been a rather sharp rise. As for the induction of foreign technology, that introduced in the 1950's was largely of a fundamental or elementary character, but in the 1960's the proportion of end-technology increased. Considering such developments in the trade of technology, we may well say that the Japanese technological standard caught up with the international level in the mid-1960's, almost ten years after the start of technological innovation in earnest. I think this fact reveals itself clearly in the structure of Japan's international balance of payments. What, then, are the characteristics of Japanese technology which have enabled it to reach the international level on the whole?

The first thing to be noted is Japan's proficiency in adopting and improving technology, which compensates for its weakness in developing basic technology.

I would like to cite the transistorized television or radio as an example. The basic technology of manufacturing the transistor was not developed in our country, but introduced into Japan from the Western Electric Company. However, it was quite impossible to use the imported transistor, as it existed at that time, for household appliances such as radio and television. In the face of this difficulty, an idea was born to adapt the technology of the transistor to fill the increasing market demand for smaller radios and televisions. Continuous efforts were made to add improvements which overcame, one by one, the technical difficulties of developing a new type of radio and television. This can be regarded as one of the best examples of the characteristics of technology in Japan.

Japanese excellence in adopting and improving technology can be attributed to the fact that Japanese technology was for some time in the process of catching up with the advanced level of foreign countries, and basic research and technology conducted in universities did not, in all cases, meet the actual needs of industry. It can also be attributed to a feature of the Japanese — we are skillful in using freely the given formula to solve problems, but are not good at inventing a formula.

The second characteristic to be noted is that we excel in the field of systems technology; that is to say, by assembling techniques of different sorts, we create an overall technology which can perform a new function. The example best manifesting the essence of Japanese systems technology is our new express train. This runs between Tokyo and Osaka, a distance of about 500 kilometers, in only three hours or so. It is true that a separate technology, such as the system for the supply and control of large amounts of electric power, the design of high-speed coaches, and the development of ATC and CTC, can boast a high level of technology; but what should be noted here is that the know-how from three different fields was coordinated into one system to effect a high-speed, safe, and comfortable railway line.

The fact that the Japanese are this good at systems technology shows that they are talented in adaptation and improvement, but at the same time it reveals their national characteristic of being able to concentrate all powers on a given purpose.

69

Future Needs

I would like, next, to refer to what the aim of future technological development in Japan should be and how it should be carried out, taking due account of the Japanese technological characteristics I have mentioned so far.

Before considering the future technological development, however, I would like to clarify what is expected today of technology. I think that lately the needs for technology have been gradually changing. I do not mean to say that the traditional objective of increasing productivity and producing new commodities filling new functions (in other words, the commercial objective) has been discarded; but the needs for technology have now become more extensive. To elaborate, technology today is urged to meet broad social needs, such as contributing to the national welfare and protecting the environment.

Therefore, in carrying out the development of technology in the future, we must first consider how we can meet such social needs. In order to make technology harmonize with social needs, we must not only add improvements to existing technology, but also combine separate technologies so as to meet the social needs. As a springboard for this goal, we can make use of the characteristics of technology in Japan today along with the past achievements in technology development. Japan should make efforts to further improve know-how and systems technology in order to get the most out of it.

However, as social needs become complex and varied, and since time for their fulfillment is short, I am afraid that it will eventually become impossible to satisfy them through small-scale and limited technological development — that is, through traditional technological improvement and its systematization in enterprises. It has now become necessary to concentrate scientific knowledge and technology, aiming at the development of basic theory and technology as well as new ways of searching for new ideas.

Since the mid-1960's, the lack of development of such elementary and theoretical technology has been recognized in Japan, and enterprises have now established their own research institutes with the intention of undertaking basic studies. But, as I have mentioned already, development of technology from now on will not be so easy for enterprises. Accordingly, it is important to reinforce research efforts by industry and, at the same time, to strengthen the interrelation between fundamental scientific studies carried out in universities and the technological research executed by enterprises.

In the past, it has been rare in Japan for fundamental studies to be coupled with technological application. And, in fact, there have been a number of cases in which Japanese-originated technology was completed overseas and then imported back into our country. In the future, however, we should try to achieve a closer relationship between fundamental science and technology, and thus make it possible for technology to respond rapidly to social needs.

It would, of course, be difficult for Japan to solve the future technological problems alone. In this connection, it is obviously imperative that international exchange of technology be increased. Japan is quite conscious of the necessity for revising the relationship between foreign and Japanese technology: we must free ourselves from passive technological development dependent on foreign technology and carry out technological interchange with foreign countries on equal terms of "give and take." And, of course, the necessity for cooperating in technological interchange is felt not only by Japan, but by every country.

For instance, the development of pollution-free automobiles would be extremely difficult without the coordination of simultaneous efforts in different fields, such as improvements in the engine, exhaustion, and fuel systems. Yet an endeavor by a single country to develop antipollution technology in every field would be difficult and wasteful. No country alone will have sufficient resources to respond adequately to the impending social

71

need for pollution-free automobiles. The need is for countries to share the responsibility in different technological areas. Each country should try to complete its own system of technology for pollution-free automobiles by integrating the results of different countries in accordance with its own specific regulations and other social needs.

Thus, in order to satisfactorily discharge the social responsibilities increasingly required of technology in the future, we must achieve an international division of technology, wherein each country takes a field where it has a comparative advantage and combines the results systematically to best serve the given purpose.

Japan intends to participate positively in such an international division of technology, making the most of the technological strengths I have referred to and eliminating her traditional attitude which called for taking advantage of foreign technology without giving in return. In light of our present high level of technology and the prospects for the future, I am convinced that this new approach is feasible and that, by so doing, Japan will contribute to the future development of international technology and the world economy.

4

How Can European Companies Maximize Effectiveness in Establishing a U.S. Position?

By KURT RICHEBÄCHER
Director, Dresdner Bank AG

A

TTEMPTS to penetrate into the economic problems of the United States have in the past produced some impressive ideas and highly plausible forecasts which later turned out completely wrong. There was a British professor convincing us in the late 1950's of the existence of a constant dollar gap. His book came out just in time for the first great dollar crisis at the beginning of the 1960's. A bit later, a thorough study by the Brookings Institution revealed basic forces at work, making for a new, substantial improvement in the basic balance of payments of the United States. Some years later, then, Monsieur Servan-Schreiber perplexed us with his "défi américain," destroying European self-confidence to the root by his discovery of a multitude of gaps between pioneering, gigantic American companies and their fragmented European counterparts. There was a technological gap, a research gap, a management gap, and . . . I do not know how many other gaps. Excuse my twisted introduction to the subject. But these recollections, I hope, make it clear that to err with respect to the Americans and to the American economy is human.

American direct investments in Europe last year exceeded a book value of $24 billion — against a book value of European investments in the United States of around $9.5 billion, up since 1967 by about 50%. In these European figures, however, British insurance companies — whose earnings record in the United States is a disgrace — loom large, with financial assets of $2 billion. Traditional European investors in the United States besides the U.K. are Switzerland and the Netherlands. Together, they account for more than 80% of European direct investment in the United States.

An outstanding novelty in the picture is the rapidly rising involvement of German companies, which — for reasons well known — had to start from scratch after the war. There were good reasons, I think, for the often-criticized policy of the Ger-

75

mans of concentrating on exports rather than on local manufacturing in other countries — and, in particular, in the United States. In many industries, for the sake of economies of scale, German companies had to build units of optimal size first. Because the domestic market was generally far too small to absorb this capacity, considerable exports were required. In this particular respect, European companies always differ fundamentally from most American companies, which have a large domestic market.

The pattern of U.S. infiltration by Europeans — as one author has characterized this process — is in many ways different from the American invasion of Europe. American companies often crash into a market, playing out their corporate size and immense financial resources.

In the early days, American foreign investment tended to concentrate on capital-intensive productions, such as vehicles, chemicals, and electrical and mechanical engineering. Moreover, the production techniques of these industries were of decisive importance. Later on, U.S. investments in Europe spread over a growing number of branches, including, more and more, service industries like banks, hotels, management consultants, and advertising agencies.

One feature common to practically all these ventures is that Americans have tended to export their American-standard products, goods, or services and their American way of corporate life, as well as their American management methods; and they usually maintain strict central control. In contrast, Europeans going to the United States share the conviction, practically to a man, that it is an indispensable prerequisite to adapt all the way to the environment, both in management methods and in marketing. So they bring their European technology and research and services, but clothed in American wrapping.

Indeed, it is research and technology that give many Europeans their competitive edge in the American market. Immense American military, electronic, and space research have, in the eyes of many Europeans, created a distorted picture of the depth and breadth of American research efforts. According to one expert, leadership in these glamorous industries has tended to conceal a narrowness of the research base. In many other fields where technical specialization and know-how play an important competitive role — as, for example, in pharmaceutical products, fibers, plastics, and machinery — European research and technology seem generally no less, if not more, efficient. In fact, many European companies devote a greater proportion of their resources to research and development.

When one looks at the rapidly lengthening list of European companies switching from exports to direct investments and local manufacturing in the United States, one is struck by the absence of many well-known European companies, whose size, specialized products, or technical expertise would seem to qualify them for the U.S. market, that have nevertheless stayed purely European, if not purely national. If they do turn up in the United States, production often is limited to a minor speciality; our most famous case here, of course, is Volkswagen. Noticeably missing in the list of European producers in the United States are the electrical concerns, though some of them certainly possess the technical strength to attack American competitors on their home ground.

Turning now to the cases of European companies that have decided to establish themselves in the United States, let us examine any common features in their approaches. Once such a firm decides to go to the United States, the first choice is between licensing an American producer and importing. It is mostly the marketing area from which Europeans shy away — and even more so, of course, when the product has to be widely distributed geographically. It takes a lot of time as well as investment to set up from scratch a sales and service organization covering a wide area. For the sales part, therefore, it is a common practice to join forces with an American trading company to which one may eventually decide to assign some specialists.

Such an arrangement is highly advantageous as a first step. There is simply no better way to test a market without incurring immediate capital commitments or capital risks. Almost as a rule, however, after a time these arrangements with intermediaries become dissatisfying to a successful and aggressive European producer. Licenses begin to be withdrawn or withheld from new products. The story ends with the European company buying its own sales agents and then gradually expanding the existing sales organization and service facilities.

When sales have reached a certain point, the technically confident European manager will carefully compare the advantages and needs of local manufacturing and those of importing. Often he will find that the big industrial customers prefer to buy directly from producers, or at least that they will restrict their purchases from importers to a certain percentage of their total requirements. Many industrial consumers fear the incalculable threats to supplies posed by strikes. Also, the mere thought that shipments of fresh supplies, which might suddenly become necessary, could take weeks and even months has a deterring effect.

Nearly all European companies producing in the United States prefer to import a range of products which they continue to manufacture at home; however, they are pretty sure that their general image of being a local producer helps them with sales of imports as well. Any such company selectively draws on the entire line of the parent company. If sales fare well and future prospects seem bright enough, replacement by local manufacture in the United States becomes a relatively easy decision.

This strategy — to start small and to move gradually from imports plus sales offices, to more elaborate service facilities, to local manufacture — is, of course, a time-consuming process. Most of our American friends do not hesitate to call it the hard way of solving the problem. Hard it certainly is in terms of patience. Whether it is also hard in terms of costs — that is where many Europeans disagree. Besides, when assessing a venture, not in retrospect but in advance, possible costs always have to be weighed against risks. The control of risks is at least as important as the control of costs.

Invasions by European Companies

Nevertheless, there may sometimes be good, or even compelling, reasons to plunge into U.S. operations on a larger scale. If so, two basic principles of approach suggest themselves: one is to set up a joint subsidiary with an American partner, with both sides swapping their particular skills and products. The other method is to buy one's way into the American market, starting, perhaps, with a participation.

In the case of both strategies, there are a number of well-known and spectacular examples. As for joint ventures:
—Bayer teamed up with Monsanto to establish Mobay.
—Hoechst joined with Hercules Powder to set up Hystron.
—Basf went into a venture with Dow Chemical.
—Rhône-Poulenc joined with Philips in another venture.

As for takeovers, it is no longer news when a European company swallows an American one. For instance:
—Olivetti bought Underwood.
—Basf purchased Wyandotte.
—ICI acquired Atlas.
—Pêchiney bought Howmet.
—British Petroleum acquired Sohio.

What are the relative merits of these two strategies?

To start with joint ventures, experience contains one point of consensus: frequently this form of partnership is unavoidable and even preferable in order to spread and to limit the risks for a major operation. But after some time, such marriages are bound to run into trouble and strife. Conflicts of interest arise

79

between the partners. Particularly in branches in which the range of products is constantly subject to change, such as chemicals, some constraint is bound to arise in the development of new products. Sooner or later, the marriage of convenience ends by the European partner buying the American out.

How do the two partners usually divide up responsibility? The American partner, with his knowledge of local conditions, will logically take charge of marketing, labor relations, and often also of production, while the European partner often delivers the greater part of product expertise and technology.

Now for the second alternative, going it alone. Is it wise for a European company to enter the American market by acquiring a substantial company with all the desired skills in products, marketing, or management? Up to now, cases of this kind have been extremely limited, and there is some reason to assume that they will remain exceptions to the rule.

In particular cases, there may be really good reasons for following this path, but few people in Europe actually consider it the ideal method. First of all, large takeovers still are at variance with the business philosophy of a good many European companies, even those of major size. Secondly, in the majority of cases, this method is not only expensive, but also highly risky. Too often, the corporate gem bought at 20 or more times annual earnings turns out as a great disappointment. Olivetti had a very bad time with Underwood, and so have some other companies with their purchases. Even if the profit record of a company is rather poor, it goes for a fancy price in the United States. Prices for companies with brilliant profit performances are out of sight.

The European bidder also realizes that he will rarely develop the sometimes-necessary ruthlessness toward the management of the absorbed company that is so often displayed by American companies in Europe. This hesitancy may well impede progress, since close collaboration with the parent company, without doubt, is of decisive importance. In addition, he is, rightly or wrongly, under the impression that dealing with American minority shareholders and the Securities and Exchange Commission poses delicate problems. Inasmuch as the family-owned company has become nearly extinct in the United States, there is hardly a company to be had without some complications in this respect.

In considering the obstacles, we must, of course, never overlook antitrust regulations. Both mergers and acquisitions call for minute examination by the SEC, which attempts to preserve competition for single products. In some cases the European company has found that these regulations hampered the control of its subsidiary. Most Europeans have realized and willynilly accepted the fact that it is simply hopeless to rely on the advice of anybody in his field, whether legal advisers or authorities. What has been smiled on for years may suddenly become the object of an antitrust attack.

For example, as long as Mobay, the joint subsidiary of Monsanto and Bayer, was working at a loss, the Justice Department kept quiet. However, just as soon as success or earnings presented themselves, critical antitrust eyes opened wide. Success can subsequently be used to refute an earlier argument of weakness. In 1962, seven years after the Bayer-Monsanto partnership, Mobay, was formed, the court ruled that Bayer should have entered the U.S. market for Mobay's major product by itself, and Monsanto was forced to sell its stake.

In examining the experience of various companies entering the U.S. market, it appears that there is no easy and quick way to gain sizable sales. The form of entry may not turn out to be the most decisive factor. It is quite common for a multiproduct company to develop a number of separate interests at first — joint ventures, licensing agreements, and imports, as well as wholly owned production and marketing facilities. Over time the ambitious company will make every effort to develop a comprehensive strategy for the whole area and the vast market, knitting together components in order to offer a fuller package and to increase overall effectiveness. In some cases it was this kind of concept which led the European company to speed the construction of a more solid and sound basis by acquiring a larger American company. The crucial thing is to determine which products are more suitable for local manufacture than for imports or licensing.

If there is one feature common to all European invaders, it is that their success nearly always rests on specialization. Seldom do they put themselves into the market for "mainstream" products. There are exceptions, of course. However, in exploring the biggest and most powerful single national market in the world, where nearly half of the world's industrial products are sold, European direct investors mainly follow the formula of aiming at a clearly specified segment of the market, whether technological or regional in nature. With a market of such dimensions, even relatively small segments offer considerable potential for growth, at least by European standards. But then, of course, other companies have to go for the market as a whole, and we have representatives of some of these kinds of companies on our panel. As Frank Schaeffer, the U.S. Department of Commerce senior official who is trying to attract foreign investment into the United States, once characterized the American market:

"Foreigners are used to thinking that every firm in our country is a national firm and a giant. They are slowly understanding that the American market and American business in reality are more fragmented, and have proportionately more small units than is usual in Western Europe."

If business seeks increasing returns on whatever research and technology are available by spreading costs over as large a sales volume as possible, the American market recommends itself simply by its size and purchasing power. Theoretically, a European company might decide to manufacture in the United States even if, on balance, net profit margins would be lower than on direct imports. There could be other compensating advantages. But many of the companies, perhaps most of the companies, going to the United States obviously did expect and achieve relatively higher profit margins in the longer run. Indeed, profit margins in the United States, on the whole, appear considerably higher than in Europe.

There may be some illusions or prejudices about the strength of competition on the two sides of the Atlantic. Americans putting their feet on European soil tend to see cartels all over the place, while the U.S. market has the image of antitrust. Some business people in Europe take quite a different view about the real situation. In their opinion, American companies do occasionally indulge in cutthroat price competition, but mainly outside their own market. In their home market they tend to preserve profit margins.

Motives and Deterrents

Initially the decision to manufacture in the United States is quite frequently taken as a protection against a multiplicity of import barriers. Outright tariffs may play a minor role, but there are many other instruments employed by the Americans to effectively restrict imports.

For example, European dyestuff producers have been driven to operate directly in the United States by the notorious American selling price system, whereby U.S. Customs assesses import tariffs on certain chemicals on the basis of ruling U.S. list prices, and not on import prices. For pharmaceutical manufacturers, the American Pure Food and Drug Administration has another whip. Since the Administration does not accept the results of testing done outside the United States, manufacturers have to maintain laboratories inside the country that duplicate similar facilities in Europe or other areas. Under various headings there are also national as well as state and local "Buy American" provisions.

Since 1962, furthermore, the number of goods put under import quotas, including voluntary restraints by foreign suppliers, shows a rising trend, not to speak of the latest currency measures and the introduction of the import surcharge.

Another reason often fairly high up in the motive list for manufacturing in the United States is nearness to customers and, consequently, increased responsiveness to local market demands in the sales, services, product development, and research areas. In many cases, changes need to be made to make a product suitable for the U.S. market. Customers often pressure the producer to locate production facilities near them. Where products are based on constant research, European companies find it useful to get support from their American research departments as a listening post sensitive to local conditions and having access to research done inside the United States. Moreover, a good local staff can meet customer needs more efficiently.

One of the traditional deterrents for direct investments in the United States is the high level of wages. In evaluating comparative costs, one has to look in two directions: local competitiveness and costs at home. The decision is made easier by the fact that manufacturing in the United States is normally for that market only. Here it may often be possible to find a location where wages are regionally lower than those which competitors are paying in other areas of the country. Indeed, there exists quite a regional differentiation in wage levels. Social Security taxes, on the other hand, are considerably higher in Europe, and in some areas of the United States — for example, in the Carolinas, in the mid-South — total costs are hardly above those in Germany.

Taxes as well as depreciation allowances compare favorably with the situation in at least some of the European countries — Germany in particular — if profits are ploughed back.

European opinion about access to finance in the United States varies considerably. Big companies find it easy to get credit from New York banks, but these banks may not be interested in transactions of less than $1 million. The European investor who approaches an American bank should be prepared to encounter an inflexible and unwilling partner.

The European company that has decided to produce in the United States can expect to receive a lot of help from the state or regional authorities. A number of these authorities are doing everything possible to bring in foreign investment. Some of them offer a bewildering variety of local inducements, beginning, but not ending, with information on financing, taxes, transportation, markets, labor supply, raw material, sites, law, regulations, and so on.

There are still many companies in Europe whose technology and research give them a chance to enter the American market profitably and successfully. Recent experience admittedly has been overshadowed by the recession and by the massive cutbacks and setbacks in aircraft industries and government spending on space and defense. For example, just before the cutbacks started, Plessey had the bad luck to buy a large manufacturer of aircraft components. Such misfortunes happen everywhere, and they remind us that there are many traps and many aspects to be taken into consideration.

Lately, European banks have begun to rush to New York. We shall see how they will fare. The bankers who made this decision have been persuaded by one particular argument which may or may not impress you. The argument is: we can no longer afford *not* to be in New York.

Following Dr. Richebächer's address, Dean Fouraker introduced the panel of authorities who would discuss various points in the address. They were:

A.W.J. Caron, *Vice Chairman of Unilever N.V.*

Gianluigi Gabetti, *General Manager, Istituto Finanziario Industriale*

G. Kraijenhoff, *President of AKZO*

MR. CARON.

Dr. Richebächer has pointed out a significant investment gap: whereas U.S. investment in Europe amounts to $24 billion, European investment in the United States amounts to $9.5 billion (including $2 billion of financial assets owned by insurance companies). Presumably this gap could be diminished if the Europeans became stronger and more efficient.

Let us first take a look at the differences between what I would call the American and the European "power houses." The concept of the "power house" implies a competitive advantage, in some sectors at least, and if we compare the American and European "power houses," we see quite a few differences.

There would of course be no point in entering the U.S. market unless one had a unique proposition and thereby an edge on competition. Now, this morning we examined the areas of R&D. We saw that the Americans have had a big lead, and although the lead may be diminishing a bit, I'm afraid that it is still very important. Also, the United States will no doubt try in future years to increase its pace and increase its lead by changing the priorities for R&D. It will be difficult, I think, for Europe to catch up with this lead, although our pace may now be a little faster.

But it is not only R&D at which we as businessmen must look. We also must look at management techniques. I find that here, again, the United States is in the lead. This is probably a function of being the biggest market in the world, and the United States has had this benefit for many decades. It provides a lead in marketing approaches to problems, administrative systems, and computer applications. It leads to advances in organization structures and advertising; and especially — because of the American character — to superior commercialization of R&D. We may be catching up there somewhat, but I think that our characters and our cultures are different, and this may explain why they are much better at the commercialization of research and development.

It is quite a revelation when one comes to the U.S. market and compares the differences in the way things are usually done there with European ways. The first thing which hits you is the size of the market, again, and the many more experts which a sizable business can draw on to help its management in preparing decisions. Also, the rate of change in business is far greater in America than it is in Europe, although we are catching up. The American consumer likes to try out innovations and does that with much more gusto, I would say, than the European consumer does.

Last, but not least, in this gap affair between the United States and Europe, I want to mention management education. Here, too, the United States has had a long lead. After all, the Harvard Business School started in 1906, and Rotterdam started a small business school in 1970. So that is a lead of about 64 years.

I think it was Robert McNamara who said that management is really the gate through which change — technological, social, or political — is distributed over society in every direction. If this concept of management is right, and, personally, I fully agree with it, then it is management education in which we have to be much better than we have been so far. It may well be that at present we've got too many scientists in the world, but I am sure that in Europe we are short of first-class business managers; we are still far behind the United States.

My conclusion would be that Europe and the United States are not yet equal partners, and that this makes it difficult to bridge the investment gap. Dr. Richebächer was right when he pointed out that investment in the United States is easier for the small and medium-sized firms. These companies don't catch the eye of the antitrust boys — only when they become big and belong to the top 500 does the Department of Justice concern itself with them. But if we say that it is easier for the smaller and medium-sized firms to get a foothold in the United States, it also means that it will take much longer to bridge the investment gap. And inasmuch as America is advancing all the time, the gap may never be closed.

The second point I would like to make is that I see a need for equal treatment of foreign investments, whether U.S. investments in Europe or European investments in the United States. We have just had a press release from EEC wherein the EEC Commission has pointed out that its members have had an open-door policy for foreign investment, whereas the United States has put up many blocks on the road. There is still quite a difference in the treatment of foreign investments, which some European businessmen really feel is a discrimination against them.

Also, I would suggest that a deeper study ought to be made — we haven't had figures on this — about the profitability of the U.S. investments of Europeans and of the American investments in Europe. The publication of the EEC Commission seems to imply that the profitability of U.S. investments in Europe is high, but we have really no figures about the profitability of European investments in the United States. It may be difficult for European investors to get the same sort of return on investment that Americans achieve in Europe.

I would suggest that we look again — and a study has probably already been made, I gather, at the Harvard Business School — about the inequitable treatment of foreign investments in the United States as compared with Europe. There is a lot of difference, of course, in the antitrust legislation, and when a company becomes a little bit bigger, then, as I said, the Department of Justice really starts to get interested. There are also national and state laws in America which need harmonization. There are still many inequalities there.

We need to establish consistent legal, fiscal, and administrative laws. The same set of rules ought to apply in Europe and the United States. If the inequities could be removed, the basis would be set, I think, for more accelerated growth of European investments. But we must not expect progress to come about overnight. There are a great many handicaps to overcome. Once you are in the United States, you will find that there is a string of regional markets. While you may be successful in the East, this may not mean that you will be successful in the South. It takes hard work and many decades, I think, to establish a national business in the United States.

As a weekend golfer, I would say that we should have another look at the various traps ahead of us which we will encounter as we go along; let's not increase the handicap for the European weekend golfer who is the junior partner to the American professional. It would be a better world, I think, if we could obtain more equitable treatment of investors. It would add up to an increase in the standard of living.

The last point I would like to make concerns the mounting criticisms about multinational firms. These criticisms come from trade unions, from governments, and from opinion molders. They claim that multinational businesses are supranational. My answer to that concern would be: let governments get together and see whether they can produce a list of rules on a supranational basis. As good citizens in the multinational business world, we would be most willing to work under such a set of unified rules.

MR. GABETTI.

My comments are going to be pragmatic, because I am a professional manager, or at least I would like to believe that I am.

I do not belong to the academic world, although I have great respect for it.

My comments are also going to be personal, because they are going to be derived from my experience in running a U.S. manufacturing subsidiary of a European company. At the same time, I have compiled, during those many years in the United States, some observations about similar situations prevailing among manufacturing subsidiaries of other European companies.

I shall be addressing myself primarily to my European colleagues in the audience. What I am going to say may have particular meaning for them inasmuch as it is the result of an experience of a European in the United States. It would be a little bit foolish for me to try to define to my American colleagues their own country.

Dr. Richebächer said that Americans tend to export their standard products, goods, and services, their American way of corporate life, and their American management methods. He says that Europeans going to the United States share the conviction, practically to a man, that it is an indispensable prerequisite to adapt all the way to the environment. I would tend to agree with this statement. Let me add that most of the time the Americans are well aware of their strength, size, and means.

In addition, Americans are strong because they have operating standards. I do not know if anyone could say that European standards exist. In Europe, there is still a variety of national standards on all grounds, including those which affect personal lives. I do feel that these barriers, which sometimes are used as an excuse for not doing things, can only be removed through a truly united Europe. Otherwise, it will always be a matter of each individual European nation trying to face that giant which is the United States — a giant united by the same language as well as by great similarity of standards within the nation.

Dr. Richebächer also stated that one deterrent to a European company becoming a producer in the United States is the Americans' fear of the incalculable threat to supplies which might be presented by strikes or other events. In my experience as a European working in the United States, I found this very often to be true. There were fear, distrust, and concern on the part of American customers with regard to the European supplier. They felt that when goods had to come from a place in the middle of nowhere, which they could only see on the map, and be subject to strikes on both sides of the ocean, the European company was not going to make a very reliable supplier.

I think that they are right. In my opinion, this is one good reason, among others, for Europeans who are interested in the American market, who are producing a large amount of goods for that market, to become manufacturers in the United States.

It is also true, however, that this does not have to be done for the full range of the product line. Once a certain relationship, a certain confidence, is established, some products which are a part of the entire assortment can still be imported and sold to the same people, who will accept them in good faith because they have seen good faith on the part of one who has made the effort to become part of the American scene.

Dr. Richebächer has indicated that there are two basic methods with which to approach the American market. One is to set up a joint subsidiary with an American partner, and the other method is to buy one's way into the American market — starting, perhaps, with a participation. This is a really key question. Here, again, I would tend to agree with what he said, that perhaps, in the long run, the best solution is to do it alone, little by little. I think that this is probably more congenial to the European way of operating.

First of all, the idea of merging the subsidiary of a European entity with an American entity is in itself a very delicate proposition. It *is* a difficult marriage, to start with. There may be a willingness to cooperate at the top level on both sides, but it is very difficult for that feeling to grow throughout the entire group of people involved. Like all marriages, the partners should share, from the very beginning, the same purposes for a long-time association. But most of the time it appears that there is some root, a germ, of conflict that could be detected at the very beginning because the purposes are different. I'm not trying to make a general statement, because, as I said, this statement is the result of personal observations of only a limited number of cases; but I would say that *most* of the time such associations are not the kind which will last for a long time.

It is often true that there is reluctance on the part of European management to suddenly terminate the management on the other side. The Europeans feel a mixture of loyalty and dependence; this can only prolong a crisis.

I agree, too, with what was said on the point of antitrust regulations. If a European company has a U.S. subsidiary which has to coexist with an American company, it is extremely important to keep the subsidiary at arm's length from the Americans. Otherwise the two firms are bound to enter into a conspiracy, and they will be prosecuted by the Department of Justice if they become large and successful.

However, I would like to say that in my 12 years of experience in the United States, I never experienced any case, any instance, of discrimination against us as the European representatives of a European company. We might have found it extremely difficult to operate under a set of circumstances, rules, and regulations which were not congenial to us because we did not learn them at school. But we tried to make an effort to learn them, and we were able to gain necessary and valuable assistance from American professionals.

If I had to offer an additional comment with regard to how a European firm can maximize its effectiveness in establishing a U.S. position, I would probably try to set aside the question of *why* the company has decided to do business in America. I would try instead to answer the question of *how* to optimize its position.

In my opinion, the best way to do this is to concentrate on the people involved, because I believe the venture will be successful or unsuccessful according to the people engaged in the venture,

92

unless the organization really is ill conceived. Certainly, a knowledge of the language is a prerequisite. Language difficulty could become a tremendous barrier for the man and for his family as well. Professionally, of course, the man has to be extremely well equipped; and, first of all, he must be very knowledgeable about his own company. Often people are sent to a foreign country — in this case we are talking about the United States — with a feeling of a special mission to perform, or to study a given question, and they will only be conversant on certain aspects of their own business or their own company. This might be enough in itself to limit their effectiveness.

The cultural factor probably is the most important. Companies should have people who are interested in cultures other than their own, who are curious about attitudes which originate from a completely different tradition and which cannot be easily modified by the personal whim of the men who are on the scene. Here, again, one has to be very careful because sometimes, not very often, even European companies will try to apply the company book. There are people who try to apply the company book to the letter in the United States. Every time that I have seen this happen, the project failed. The Europeans must be willing to rewrite the company book according to the requirements, the laws, and the customs of their local environment.

What policies will help to this end? I believe that, first, one should send a competent staff — a staff which also loves the country and is willing to stay there. Secondly, the staff should be willing to establish a clearly identifiable base so that anyone in the United States who wants to enter into a relationship with that specific company can find competent representatives at that base, and not just people who go back and forth, spending more time on airplanes than at the subsidiary just to avoid the correspondence. Third, I would say that the base should be one to which the executives from Europe can come to learn and operate. The Europeans should not just come for some parties or social visits.

93

I am a great believer in the multinational company. I believe that governments should get together and define the status and role of this type of enterprise. I believe that as long as it is only the expression of one single nationality, it will not be brought into being. In my opinion, the real secret of success for a multinational company is to have local nationals heading operations. This is the only way, in my opinion, to create the new business citizens of the world.

MR. KRAIJENHOFF.

We have been in general agreement on the main issues thus far, so I shall try purposely to raise some fresh questions and issues.

First, may there not be a logical reason for the investment gap between Europe and the United States? I believe the gap is not based on technological advance alone. The European market has grown to such an extent that it not only has become an attractive investment climate for the American firms, but it has used up all the cash roll of the European companies trying to keep their shares in it. This, of course, has made it very difficult for European companies to seek overseas opportunities at the same time.

The fact that the growth is now slowing down somewhat makes it all the more sad that, at this moment, the resources of the European companies are not such that they can afford to take "the big leap forward" across the ocean. However, I feel that it is not logical to say that we will never be able to bridge that gap. In view of the present recession we are in, and which will no doubt get worse, the only thing we can see that we will have missed is the full use of all the opportunities that are there. It is essential for any company wanting to tackle the U.S. market to have sufficient financial strength to be able to face some setbacks. If you are unable to weather setbacks, you had better stay out.

The idea of going on one's own with a small market penetration is viable only if you have a patented technology which is

94

highly superior, and which gives you the time to really get your foothold in the U.S. market. Such situations are rare, however. Therefore, I would claim that the best way to get started in the United States would be to acquire an American company, if you can. Then, even if you have acquired 100% control, put it on the stock market again to make it a real American company.

I know that there are different schools of thought — people who say that the best way to run a multinational operation, particularly a technology-based multinational operation, is to have completely owned subsidiaries. I don't believe that. I think that in the long run it is better to be thoroughly integrated into a local market, particularly if it is as sophisticated a market as that in the United States.

I also believe that any company wanting to go into the United States in a big way has to be listed on a major stock exchange, and has to have Americans among its top management, if it wants to attract high-caliber American talent. The Dutch have always believed in being listed on the U.S. exchanges, but the Germans and Swiss have not. Also, there are very few big British companies in the stock market in the States. Beecham has now done this, of course, but in general you will find that even a company like ICI has only recently made its first big move. In its big fiber business it works together with Celanese in a minority position, and recently it acquired Atlas.

I think other problems have affected our investment gap. Mergers or acquisitions involving an exchange of shares have been very difficult to accomplish. This is partly the result of difficulties with the price/earnings ratio, as was already mentioned, and partly because of the interest-equalization tax. This brings me to the subject of inequalities.

The inequalities stem not only from the fact that we have to pay an interest-equalization tax, but also from the fact that some local taxes and rulings make it impossible for us to invest in certain types of industries. Furthermore, we are subject to various fiscal and legal requirements, which can also vary locally.

Another problem is that we never know where we are with the Department of Justice. Now, I must say that, in our case, we have been pretty well treated by the Department of Justice; but I can cite a few instances where, I think, it would be difficult to explain just why people were made to do what they were.

Take the CIBA-Geigy merger, which is a merger formed outside the United States by two companies which had subsidiaries inside the United States. These companies were forced to divest part of their business; they held only 2% of the market in that business. This is, for us, somewhat difficult to understand. The biggest company in their field has 6% of the market, so you can't really talk about a dominating position. Yet divestiture was made a condition of acceptance for the merger. So what CIBA had to do was to sell off part of its product line to Revlon, in exchange for a few other products. Naturally, it is a handicap for a European company to enter the U.S. market without knowing what it may have to sell when it gets established!

Another troublesome case is that of British Petroleum and Sohio. It is true, though, that in Ohio the U.S. firm did hold a tremendous market share.

If the European management decides it cannot acquire a U.S. company by an exchange of shares, might it arrange a "reverse takeover"? This would mean that a *division* of the European company would be taken over by a U.S. company, thus making the European parent a shareholder in the American firm. Unfortunately, this makes the European company subject to the rulings of, first of all, the Department of Justice. Also, its investments in that particular division would have to come up before the Investment Board in Washington. Such a move would limit the mobility of the European company, which in that case would probably still have its main activities outside the United States. This is another reason why investments in the U.S. market are being limited.

Let's look at the general return on investment. Consider, first, what has happened to the return on investment in the 200

96

biggest European companies: in ten years it has gone down from 5.7% after taxes to 3%. Now, the return on investment in U.S. companies in comparable types of business is usually about 40% higher than ours. I think this is partly due to the fact that we in Europe have grown up with the idea that market share is the magic thing. We think that if we have market share, we have profits. The United States has had to live with a regime which is much more difficult, particularly if a company's market share grows. Perhaps partly because of these U.S. restrictions, Americans have become much more profit-conscious than we are. And they accept what is called "price leadership," which also is something we Europeans apparently have some problems with.

Following Mr. Kraijenhoff's talk, Dean Fouraker opened the discussion to the members of the audience, inviting questions for the panelists and Dr. Richebächer. Portions of the ensuing dialogue are reproduced here.

OTTO J. DAX (SIEMENS CORPORATION, U.S.A.).

I would like to say that I agree with Dr. Richebächer's comments. His description of the situation in the United States expresses exactly how I feel after more or less three years' experience there.

There was one remark of Mr. Gabetti's, however, that I disagree with. He said that there is no discrimination in the United States. I would like to ask a simple question — that is, whether or not the "Buy American" Act is a form of discrimination. I have two or three big businesses now, and I cannot sell in the United States because the requirement is that company headquarters have to be in the United States, and the product has to be at least 50% of U.S. origin. The customer wants our product. The customer needs it because it's a product which doesn't exist in the United States, and the customer likes us because our service is better than our competitors' service. The question here is whether or not the "Buy American" Act is a form of discrimination.

MR. GABETTI.

I must say, first of all, that I did not work in the United States after August 15, 1971, so I don't know exactly how the situation is now. I also indicated that I had been in charge of the manufacturing operations of the manufacturing subsidiary of a European company. I did say that, during my experience, we never saw any specific discrimination against us. But, in effect, we were manufacturing in the United States. My point was that, as foreigners conducting a manufacturing operation in the United States, we were never discriminated against.

MR. KRAIJENHOFF.

I personally think that Mr. Dax is right. The practice described is discrimination, just as the "DISC" legislation is.

DEAN FOURAKER.

As an American, I would have to agree; and, as an economist, I must say that there is no question it is not an act of free trade. The question of balancing one form of discrimination against perceived forms in other markets is what is at issue. But the "Buy American" Act is certainly not a means of facilitating a free exchange.

I have a question for these panelists that affects Dr. Riche-bächer as well. I believe that well over a third of the exports of the United States now are those made by parent companies to their subsidiaries, and approximately the same ratio of imports are from subsidiaries to parents of international companies. The trend seems to be rising very rapidly. Most of the trade in the future in the United States may be within the institutions of international companies. Do you see this affecting your decision to invest in the United States, and do you see this having any effect on the way Japanese business firms perceive the rest of the world? I'd be delighted to have anyone comment on this. Dr. Richebächer, was that a factor in your decision to go to New York?

DR. RICHEBÄCHER.

Our "raw material" is money. It comes from all over the world — not only from the United States, but from the international market as well. In our case, the decision was not only to go to the United States, but to use New York as a base for a much wider operation. So we are different in this respect from most of the other producers, since they generally produce only for the United States.

MR. KRAIJENHOFF.

I think it is also often the case that exports later become imports. For instance, in the case of textiles, the raw material is sent out of the country, worked up into finished goods or semifinished goods, and then returned to the country. This is the type of trade we see increasing considerably. This also happens in

Europe, where quite a lot of goods in the form of raw materials are exported from Europe to the Iron Curtain countries or Hong Kong, Morocco, and the other so-called "cheap labor" countries, and later returned in the form of finished goods.

MICHEL JALABERT (GEMINI COMPUTER SYSTEMS).

I would like to know from the panelists what, in their opinion, it is that we Europeans can bring to the United States that Americans don't already have.

MR. KRAIJENHOFF.

I think there are plenty of examples of European contributions toward new products in the United States. I think a very good example of these are the contributions made by the Swiss companies, which, as you may know, occupy a tremendous position in the pharmaceutical field in the United States. They have certainly, one might say, "let loose" the big tranquilizer business, which was initially launched by an American company. I think you will find that in many of these specialized fields, European firms have really got a very important and dominant position in the United States. This is not only true in the case of the well-known products which you recognize by their brand names, but also in a number of other fields. You will find that generally the leadership position of European firms is due to the fact that they exploited a certain segment of the market which, to many American firms, may not have been so interesting at first. This is their chance for success. I think it will continue to be so. The trend in this direction certainly is increasing.

MR. DAX.

European firms are much more willing, I think, to make equipment to customers' specifications. Big American firms prefer to sell a product only if a large market exists for it; we Europeans are much more modest. For instance, if an American professor in the medical field wants special x-ray equipment, we are willing to make it for him, and naturally that is an advantage for us. In the sophisticated x-ray field, my company has 27% of the U.S. market, and I think that is a very big percentage in this huge market.

ANTHONY PELL (TENER R. ECKELBERRY & ASSOCIATES, PARIS).

I want to go back to a point Dr. Kraijenhoff spoke about. Perhaps European managers are not sufficiently aware of the enormous vitality, even in bad times, of the U.S. capital market, which permits the technologically advanced European country or company to use a stock exchange as a vehicle for its future growth in the United States. One British insurance company, for example, recently bought a couple of companies in Hartford, Connecticut. This company is using a capital market to give it both equity and debt financing; the company wouldn't be able to find such financing on this side of the Atlantic.

In one particular case which I happen to be working on right now, a small, technologically advanced European company that has engaged in a joint venture with an American company is going to try to chip off, over a three-year period, about 5% to 7% of a market which is now largely held by a single giant. Now, the objective is to have this company go public, even though the profits are going to be small and the size of the total venture is going to be small for the first three or four years. The corporate managers figure that on the basis of what they can do through a stock exchange, they will be able to buy even larger companies than the ones they started out with. Yet at the start this company was ahead of the Americans only in technology.

MR. CARON.

I think you are quite right. If you look at the price/earnings ratios of the foreign multinationals on the New York Stock Exchange, you will see these are a reflection of our low price/earnings ratio in Europe. If you then look at one of these multinational's subsidiaries in the United States, you will see that if one put that company on the stock market, its price/earnings share would be 2.5 to 3 times that of the mother company's in Europe and in the United States. So I quite agree with you that the stock market provides an enormous possibility to raise finance.

MR. HAWRYLYSHYN.

There was a question raised that I found very interesting. The question was: Can Europe — and maybe I can add Japan — bring something to the United States?

I think that one of the things Europe and Japan could contribute is some changes in the management style in the United States that might make it somewhat more compatible with the new value system that one sees emerging in the United States, as manifested by some of the younger generation there.

While I cannot take as much time as I would like to develop the topic, I would like to say that, certainly in Japan and in some countries in Europe, there is a great capacity to work in groups, in teams — cooperation versus competition within firms and within groups. When rewards are not tied too closely to individual performance, there is more willingness to cooperate. We find that typified in Japan.

I find that the same thing is happening among the younger people in the United States. One of the reasons they are rejecting the business culture as it has evolved is that it has been too much of the dog-eat-dog variety — too much competition, too much individualism in it. We sense it even from young Americans who have come over to Europe for management courses. They still want competition, but they want it within groups, not individuals. They say, "Put us into groups, and then let groups compete against other groups; but don't give us assignments that make us compete against each other. Individually we don't want to do well if it requires pushing someone else down."

I think the Japanese have something in their teamwork from which we in Europe can learn a bit, and, I think, from which the United States can learn quite a bit. Business could be made much more compatible with the rising values of the youth culture.

A second point I would like to make relates to the findings of a two-year study we have just completed at CEI on European business strategies in the United States, or on how to manage European subsidiaries in the United States. Samples were taken from among 49 European firms with subsidiaries in the United States. One of the most surprising findings was that among causes of failure is the placing of management of the U.S. subsidiary entirely in the hands of American managers. I was surprised because, you know, U.S. management know-how is so often considered superior.

We have some tentative explanations as to why this is so. For one thing, to move into the United States successfully, a company needs some kind of superiority in processes or products, some sort of technical lead to get in. If the know-how has to be updated, or if fresh know-how has to flow into the United States from headquarters, it would seem that a company would need some Europeans in the subsidiary top management to ensure the flow. Otherwise, the pipeline would be constricted.

Even when the U.S. affiliate has grown so large that it has become the source of innovation in know-how for company operations all over the world, the subsidiary still needs Europeans in the top management team if it is to ensure the flow of know-how in the *opposite* direction. Otherwise, there will be a great deal of resentment at headquarters that this "daughter," if you wish, has become so big that she is trying now to manage the parent company.

I must add that, conversely, we find the company must have some Americans, too, within the management team in the U.S. operation, particularly in the marketing area. Otherwise the company does not do too well.

I mention these findings because they have startled me and, I think, startled some others. I wonder whether we could have some comments on how the European company's organizational structure should evolve with time in order not only to gain a position in the United States, but to continue to maximize the U.S. position on a worldwide basis.

MR. GABETTI.

I tend to agree with what you say. Personally, I believe that a minimum number of Europeans should be in the subsidiary. Probably you have to start with a small group of pioneers — and again, I would recommend pioneers of top quality — and as soon as possible hire for that team just as many Americans with talent and ability as possible. This is why it is important initially to send a nucleus of Europeans with top-notch ability. Otherwise, they will hire Americans with mediocre ability to match theirs, and the company will be a failure.

I also believe that the Europeans who are going to remain in the operation do not necessarily have to hold top positions. I think they are vital, however, in those positions which are important to ensure current, reliable communication with the rest of the worldwide organization.

LORD BOWDEN.

I want to ask the panel members whether they think that the difference between the American and the European patent laws has significance in this question of technological innovation. Historically, American patent law originated with the belief that any American who went to Europe and returned with a process should be entitled to the proceeds, whether he had invented it or stolen it. Now, this tradition, which was probably absolutely right in Benjamin Franklin's time, still seems in some way to influence American patent law.

I would be interested to know if anyone who has had experience in this matter can throw any light on the effect it is having on the translation of technology between the United States and Europe.

MR. KRAIJENHOFF.

It can be very advantageous to conduct research in the United States so as to have a patent position there. The American patent laws are one of the very important reasons for a multinational business to want to be in the United States. It does not want to be caught in the position of being an inventor outside the United States.

MR. CARON.

At Unilever we have solved the problem in much the same way. We do R&D in the United States and file patents simultaneously in a number of countries. By doing this, we avoid the disruption of having our patents stolen by burglars.

DEAN FOURAKER.

I should like to thank our main speaker, Dr. Richebächer, our panelists, Mr. Caron, Mr. Gabetti, and Mr. Kraijenhoff, and our participants. I feel that this has been a most productive day. We have gained a number of different perspectives, and there has been a great deal of exchange of information about international business and international opportunities. I am persuaded that although there may be temporary interruptions, this kind of exchange is going to be a continued force toward economic integration of the industrial countries of the world. I hope to see many of you again in that process.

Thank you very much for coming.

These proceedings are adjourned.

Index